Praise for *You, Me, We*

"*You, Me, We* is about building important connections at work—and that's something we all need more of in these disconnected times. This page-turner is a playbook for how to create a mindset that will gain you allies who will not only help you get more done, but also feel better about the time you spend on the job. Let's face it, we all have negative relationships in our lives, some that may suck the very life out of us at times. The authors help you spot the bad and cultivate more of the good. And that's a skill that's worth building!"

ADRIAN GOSTICK AND CHESTER ELTON, *New York Times*–bestselling authors, *All In* and *Leading with Gratitude*

"*You, Me, We* is a must-read for anyone looking to amplify their leadership presence and impact. At the end of the day, leadership is all about creating meaningful relationships—friendships at work—and this book reveals the five practices that result in an engaged workforce and superior results for all."

GARRY RIDGE, The Culture Coach

"It is so easy to show up as a critic in our relationships. Of course, being an ally is far more effective. What makes *You, Me, We* such a great book is that Morag Barrett, Eric Spencer, and Ruby Vesely don't just acknowledge the importance of being an ally, they actually help us do it. Read this book. Put their advice into practice. Your relationships will be better for it!"

PETER BREGMAN, CEO, Bregman Partners; author, *18 Minutes* and *Leading with Emotional Courage*

"How we feel about work is wrapped up in the strength of our relationships. Learning and practicing the ally behaviors outlined in *You, Me, We* is central to creating strong, trusting, lasting relationships at work."

CARALYN COOLEY, chief people officer, Bowery Farming

"As Gallup has clearly demonstrated, having a best friend at work is integral for employees to be truly engaged with their team members to best benefit the business. But no one knew exactly how to make that happen and the factor was broadly thought to be 'inactionable.' Finally, we have the answer. *You, Me, We* shows exactly how you can promote an Ally Mindset throughout your organization and to reap the benefits of doing so. This invaluable guide on this essential topic is needed now more than ever."

BOB NELSON, PhD, world's leading authority on employee recognition and engagement; 5-million-copy–bestselling author

"This book is so very insightful and truly underlines the importance of having great friendships at work. In a world where employees are leaving their workplaces at a record pace, *You, Me, We* provides the perfect recipe to keep employees tied to organizations longer. If you are looking for ways to connect your team, reenergize them, and make them want to stay, this book is one of the best investments you can make."

HEATHER R. YOUNGER, bestselling author, *The Art of Caring Leadership*

"My personal motto is, 'Work with your friends; become friends with people you work with.' *You, Me, We* shows you why those connections are essential."

AYSE BIRSEL, award-winning industrial designer; author, *Design the Life You Love*

"We have learned how critically important the value of connection is in our lives now more than ever. *You, Me, We,* provides a clear and empowering clarion call for how we all can show up to work not just as a friend, but as an ally."

ALISA COHN, author, *From Start-Up to Grown-Up*; executive coach

"Having and being a friend at work are the essential ingredients for creating a highly engaged and productive team. *You, Me, We* is the recipe for success that not only shows you why meaningful relationships matter, but also how to cultivate an Ally Mindset to ensure mutual success. This book should be required reading for all leaders."

ROBBIE SAMUELS, author, speaker, business growth strategy coach

"Business performance and employee engagement converge when we're in the presence of allies. By adopting an Ally Mindset, the nucleus of *You, Me, We,* leaders will learn how to show up unconditionally for everyone while inspiring their teams to invest in the power of critical workplace friendships."

SHANNON SISLER, EVP and chief people officer, Crocs

"I love *You, Me, We.* It contains the three things I appreciate most: interesting stories, strong research underpinnings, and practical, applicable advice that drives success—all told in an easy-going but direct fashion. Buy extra copies. You'll want to give them to people before you've even finished reading it yourself!"

CYNTHIA BURNHAM, Master Corporate Executive Coach; leadership consultant

YOU
ME
WE

Why We All Need a Friend at Work
(and How to Show Up as One!)

MORAG BARRETT
ERIC SPENCER • RUBY VESELY
FOREWORD BY **DR. MARSHALL GOLDSMITH**

YOU
ME
WE

Cataloguing in publication information is
available from Library and Archives Canada.
ISBN 978-1-77458-203-9 (hardcover)
ISBN 978-1-77458-204-6 (ebook)

Page Two
pagetwo.com

Edited by Kendra Ward
Copyedited by Crissy Calhoun
Proofread by Alison Strobel
Jacket and interior design by Jennifer Lum
Interior illustrations by Vicari Vollmar Conley,
Jena Persico, and Setareh Ashrafologhalai
Printed and bound in Canada by Friesens
Distributed in Canada by Raincoast Books
Distributed in the US and internationally by Macmillan

22 23 24 25 26   5 4 3 2 1

YouMeWeBook.com

For love. The ultimate expression of you,
me, and when we are better together.

MORAG BARRETT

To my wonderful kiddos, Eva and Fiona. Sometimes
the similarities between organizational leadership
and parenting are uncanny! Thank you for all the stories
that you don't know that you're a part of (and for
being the amazing humans that you are)! To Lori, for
teaching me things about relationships that I never knew,
and for helping me to understand that everything
is going to be awesome! And to my folks, PK & Jane,
for teaching me a long time ago that I could
do anything I wanted... except major in music,
because "How will you make a living?" ☺

ERIC SPENCER

To Ric, my great love and fierce ally,
your belief in me moves mountains.

RUBY VESELY

CONTENTS

FOREWORD

BUILDING *REAL* CONNECTIONS with others in the workplace has always been a challenge, and this challenge has been magnified in recent times, when many of us have been pushed out of our offices and into remote work sites—often our own home offices, kitchens, or bedrooms. Gone are the in-person watercooler discussions where new ideas were sparked and relationships built. In their place are endless Zoom calls, decreased visibility, and increased isolation.

And while we hope that the forces that pushed us out of our offices will soon abate, simply putting people back into their cubicles doesn't mean that they will connect and build deep and lasting relationships again, assuming they had them to begin with. It takes much more than hope to fill in these ever-deepening relationship gaps.

So, how can leaders, and the people who work with and for them, build connections in these disconnected times, and why should they even bother?

In this insightful, thought-provoking book, Morag Barrett, Eric Spencer, and Ruby Vesely explain in detail not only why we should work intentionally and thoughtfully to build connection with others but also provide a powerful road map for how we can do it.

At the heart of *You, Me, We* is a model called the Ally Mindset, originally developed by Morag in her book *Cultivate: The Power of Winning Relationships*. The Ally Mindset is how we show up in the relationships that matter most to us. Do we build one another up or tear each other down? Over the years, I have coached executives in far too many organizations where the negative relationships have outnumbered the positive ones, and these negative relationships have caused great harm—interpersonally, financially, and in many other ways.

The Ally Mindset model comprises five practices: abundance and generosity, connection and compassion, courage and vulnerability, candor and debate, and action and accountability. To be a true ally to others, you must embody and demonstrate these practices in equal measure. And when you do, you might be surprised by the tremendously positive effect you have on those around you, both at work and in your personal life.

So, how do you know when you're in the presence of an ally?

They have the same goals you have. They are happy to be your sounding board, listening intently to your ideas and suggestions for improvement. They work with you instead of against you. They're straight shooters; they tell you the unvarnished truth. They always have your back.

Ultimately, this book is all about moving from *me* to *we*.

As the saying attributed to philosopher Lao Tzu goes, "If you do not change direction, you may end up where you are heading." Ask yourself, Where am I heading? Am I pointed in the right direction? If the answer to that last question is no, then change your course. The day we take the first step to turn our colleagues into trusted friends and allies is the day we truly begin to love our work, our companies, and our lives.

DR. MARSHALL GOLDSMITH
Thinkers50 number one executive coach and *New York Times*-bestselling author of *Triggers, Mojo,* and *What Got You Here Won't Get You There*

NOW'S THE TIME

MY HAND HOVERED over the phone as I read the name and number that stared back at me. Should I answer? Let it go to voicemail? I was conflicted. Then technology saved me: before I could pick up, the call vanished. I felt a moment of guilt. And then the little message icon popped up on my phone, and I groaned.

There would be no escape.

I knew what Fiona wanted. It was the same thing she wanted every time she called. She was going to update me on the latest soap-opera antics of her colleague. For more than a year, she'd been calling, regular as clockwork, to BMW (bitch, moan, and whine) about this coworker. It was a real Jekyll-and-Hyde relationship, and while it had been amusing at first, she was now carrying a heavy load. Her self-confidence was at rock bottom; she hated her job; she resented her colleagues; and she loathed this particular colleague most of all. She was trapped, a victim of her circumstances.

Despite our regular conversations, Fiona didn't see things that way. She focused on her colleague's transgressions and couldn't see her own part in this play. She wasn't ready (or willing) to have the tough conversations or to take ownership and show up differently to change the ending of the story. The emotional toll was heavy on her, and it was starting to impact me—as evidenced by my reluctance to answer her call.

And then it hit me.

I, too, was stuck in a pattern of behavior that no longer served me, Fiona, or our relationship. I wasn't stepping up to the tough conversations with Fiona or showing up as an ally for myself. This was my moment to look up, show up, and step up—be aware of how I want others to feel in my presence, be intentional about I show up, and do my best. To reset my relationship with Fiona and get us back on track, together.

Maybe you have a Fiona in your life, or perhaps a toxic coworker relationship similar to the one Fiona was navigating. It's hard working alongside a colleague you don't respect or who doesn't appear to respect you. Perhaps you've received tough feedback about how you relate with others or missed a promotion opportunity because you lack good relationships— denting your confidence and leaving you unsure about how to proceed. Whatever your reason for picking up this book, my SkyeTeam colleagues and coauthors, Ruby and Eric, and I have got you! While we have written this book primarily for leaders at every level of any organization, formal and informal, you'll find that the practices we outline can be used effectively by any employee.

This book shares more than a decade of research and personal life experience since my first book, *Cultivate: The Power of Winning Relationships*, was published. In that book, I shared the concept of the Relationship Ecosystem (a brief description is included in chapter 1) and introduced the Ally, Supporter, Rival, and Adversary relationships. It resonated.

That was all well and good, but we at SkyeTeam were consistently asked, "How do I show up as an ally? Both for my established relationships and with new colleagues where I may have no track record?" So, Eric, Ruby, and I set about answering that question—to identify and understand that how we feel, think, and act impacts our reputation as a go-to or go-from colleague. This was the inspiration for the Ally Mindset Profile and for the five practices we share with you in this book. The Ally Mindset Profile is a powerful tool we developed to identify your strengths and potential areas for improvement in these five practices.

Our research includes data from more than five hundred global leaders who've completed the Ally Mindset Profile (please take a moment to complete yours and add to our research here: SkyeTeam.cloud/YouMeWe), as well as insights gained in our keynotes and workshops from more than one thousand participants who lead top companies across the US and Europe. They shared what it looks and feels like when these practices are present—and when they are missing—and the impact this has on their personal and organizational success. Our research also includes the work of others in this field, along with exclusive interviews we conducted with industry leaders.

All this research, however, doesn't mean we get it right every single time. What we do know is that even with our missteps, our team at SkyeTeam is the strongest we have ever experienced. We are truly better together. And the work we do for our clients and the strong, trusting relationships we have built with them show us that an Ally Mindset really does ensure mutual success.

Now it's your turn.

Pull up a chair and pour yourself a cup of coffee as we share the secrets of the Ally Mindset with you. Now's the time to look up, show up, and step up in all your relationships—at work and at home—to multiply your leadership impact and success.

MORAG BARRETT
Founder and CEO, SkyeTeam

Introduction

RELATIONSHIPS

The True Currency for Success

I N A *Harvard Business Review* article, senior editor Alison
Beard tells a story about her very first best friend at work.
The scene was *The Free Lance-Star*, a Fredericksburg, Virginia, newspaper where she had landed a job as a freshly
minted cub reporter. The newspaper office was small—like
blink-and-you've-passed-it-by small—so it didn't take her
long to meet and get to know everyone who worked there.

After making the rounds of her new coworkers, one person
stood out: Ted Byrd, a veteran of the newspaper with whom
Alison shared much in common. They were both graduates of
Washington and Lee University; they were both runners with
a penchant for early morning workouts; and they both looked
forward to having a glass of wine at the end of a long workweek. However, writes Alison, "More important, we enjoyed
working together. We shared ideas, advice, annoyances, and
jokes. He made my professional—and personal—life better."

Though a decade apart in age, the two immediately
bonded, becoming best friends at work—supporting and elevating each other during the course of their work relationship.
After just a year at *The Free Lance-Star*, Alison left behind the
small-town newspaper and her best friend at work, Ted, as

she moved up to the big leagues—first at *Financial Times* and then *Harvard Business Review*. Not one to stay stuck in the past for very long, Alison quickly found new best friends at work at each organization—people whom she counted on to watch her back and who counted on her to watch theirs.

Throughout it all, Alison and her best friends at work all shared one important thing in common: they had an *Ally Mindset*. The Ally Mindset is how you show up in the relationships that matter most to you—whether or not the other person is showing up as an ally or a rival, a friend or an enemy. As a result, you are more likely to be engaged in these relationships rather than checked out. The Ally Mindset is the guiding principle that drives intentionality—what you feel, think, and do—and ultimately the health of the relationship and the mutual success that comes from it.

The benefits of adopting an Ally Mindset are clear and compelling. According to research conducted by Tom Rath, former Gallup global practice leader, people who have at least three close friends at work are seven times more likely to be engaged in their jobs. In addition, having best friends at work will make you 96 percent more likely to be extremely satisfied with your life, cut in half your chance of dying of heart disease, accelerate your body's ability to heal, and reduce the possibility that you'll ever suffer from ill effects of Alzheimer's disease, certain cancers, type 2 diabetes, and osteoporosis.

Not too shabby.

The problem is that given the competing demands and priorities that people are already juggling in their intense, hair-on-fire work and personal lives—exacerbated by the COVID-19 global pandemic, which has thrown everyone's lives into disarray while isolating them from their workmates—work friendships are often given short shrift. As the research shows, this lost opportunity can tremendously impact our happiness, well-being, and ultimately our success (or lack thereof).

In this book, we explore the importance of establishing close relationships at work—*friendships*—and show how to create the kind of mindset essential for making allies while delivering the business results being asked of you. We show you how to adopt the Ally Mindset so that you can be a more effective leader, improve your long-term career results, boost employee engagement, strengthen your relationships, and benefit your own health and that of others around you.

Keep in mind that we can't rely on or expect others to build these kinds of relationships with us. *We* must actively take the initiative to understand what is important to the other person while authentically sharing with others what is important to *us*. It's about saying, "Of course I'll help you," but it's also about attending to your own needs, wants, and dreams.

For those who adopt the Ally Mindset, one plus one really *does* equal three.

We are Morag Barrett, Eric Spencer, and Ruby Vesely—best friends and executives at SkyeTeam, a leadership development consultancy focused on building connection in the workplace so that individuals and teams can have a greater impact.

In our own work with clients, which range from Google to the National Geographic Society, Scholastic, Charter Communications, and many others, we have found that one of the most important indicators of individual, team, and organizational success is the presence of an Ally Mindset. When people have best friends at work—people who stick together, in good times and bad, and who help ensure everyone makes it through—they thrive. When they don't, they flail and eventually crash.

Here's an example: not all that long ago, Morag facilitated a client's all-employee event on Zoom. We're not exaggerating when we say that as the Zoom room opened, the three hundred employees came bounding in, all kinds of excited to see their work friends—some besties and some simply acquaintances—after COVID had plucked them out of the office months earlier. There were calls to each other: "Hey, I haven't seen you in ages!" "How's the dog?" "Has John fixed the leak yet?" There were in-jokes, out-jokes, and a level of banter we haven't seen in any other virtual event. Cameras were on. Everyone was fully engaged, no multitasking. The energy and enthusiasm were palpable.

One of Morag's first questions to the group was "What emotions have you, or your friends, experienced at work in the last six weeks?" The responses were telling (and eye-opening, as the CEO said to us afterward): anxious, stressed, frustrated, overwhelmed, disconnected, worried—all understandable in this uncertain time. The outward appearance of ally behaviors, of fun and frivolity, masked an underlying malaise that could have undermined the sense of team and the results they were able to achieve together. As you will learn later, this team demonstrated connection and compassion but were missing candor and debate (the ability to share their true feelings), and it was undermining the organization's success.

The social distance of working from home had caused many relationships to take a step back, increasing people's sense of disconnection from the team and organization. Individual stress and burnout levels were increasing, with the warning signs starting to appear in turnover rates and exit interview comments. A couple of key project deliverables had been missed, each team assuming that the other had responsibility for that part of the project. The rush from one online meeting to another had created the illusion of collaboration and alignment, which, had it not been identified, would have damaged the firm's reputation and client relationships.

The CEO shared with us later that the event acted as a catalyst for change for himself personally and for the organization. He reprioritized his time to intentionally focus on nurturing relationships, reconnecting across the organization, and creating opportunities at all levels to show that the organization cared about its team members as individuals. As a result, feedback through the monthly employee survey improved, and they headed off the stress and burnout that was simmering just below the surface, while increasing opportunities for collaboration and transparent accountability across teams.

In this book, we offer a systematic approach—proven over the course of many years in our research and in practice with companies of all shapes and sizes—for how you can most effectively show up at work. We show you how to take back control of your work, to speak your truth, and to be seen, heard, and valued. We give you the tools you need to nurture your work relationships with intentionality, not relying on chance or random connections. And as we continue to explore the new hybrid world of work that the COVID-19 pandemic pushed us all into, these tools and skills are more important than ever before.

We confess: we don't just preach the Ally Mindset. We live it; we breathe it. Using the Ally Mindset, we've accomplished some pretty amazing things over the past few years. *Together.* Our programs are better. Our delivery is better. Our research is better. Our relationships are better. Our lives are better.

Remember, to *have* friends, you need to *be* a friend; you need to go first. In the pages that follow, we'll show you exactly how to do that—and much more.

So, pull up a chair. Put in your earphones. Buckle up. And get ready to change your life—and the lives of those around you—forever.

Ready to get started?

Let's go!

THE REMARKABLE POWER OF BEING A FRIEND AT WORK

Why Be Robin to My Batman?

❝

Invest in relationships. Life is hard.
None of us has the strength
to do it alone. We need people to
encourage and inspire us so we can
encourage and inspire others.

SIMON SINEK

THELMA AND LOUISE. Woody and Buzz. Serena and Venus. Frodo and Sam. Ben and Jerry. Batman and Robin. These dynamic duos stick in our mind for a reason: together they accomplished truly remarkable things—far more than either individual could have accomplished alone. Sure, while some of these pairings live only in fiction, the deep bonds of friendship (dare we say, *affection*) these BFFs share—coupled with how they show up for each other through thick and thin—can inspire us to dream more, achieve more, *be* more.

Here's one of our favorite examples: Batman and Robin. The Batman character was introduced to the public in a 1939 comic book. Batman (spoiler alert! secretly he's wealthy industrialist Bruce Wayne) dedicated his life to fighting crime in Gotham City, driven by the brutal killing of his parents by a mugger. And he did just that—solo, all by himself, spectacularly. The comic book's writers quickly realized, however, that something was missing in the Batman story, and they took steps to fix it. Just one year later—in 1940—they introduced a new character to the Batman universe: Robin, the Boy Wonder.

Robin was more than a sidekick to Batman; he was his closest ally and best friend at work. He was a sounding board off which Batman could bounce ideas. He was an extra set of fists when the going got tough. He was the rock that Batman knew he could count on—always and forever. Robin had Batman's back, and vice versa. Not only that, but Robin injected a bit of humor into the proceedings. Before Robin's introduction, Batman was a dark and brooding character. That changed when Robin arrived. Batman and the Boy Wonder had more fun together than they did when they were apart.

And the writers of the Batman comics didn't stop with Robin. A few years later, in 1943, they introduced another character: Bruce Wayne's trusty valet, Alfred, who, in addition to his domestic duties, supported Batman and Robin in their crime-fighting mission by acting as a detective and taking care of business behind the scenes. Robin and Alfred were Batman's allies—they had his back, and in doing so, they allowed Batman to *be* Batman.

And that's what being an ally is. Our allies allow us to be who we are, and they help keep us grounded when we go off track.

But it's easy to be someone's Batman or Robin on the good days. The true test is when we're in the alley about to fight the villains. Who has *your* back and whose back do *you* have? This is what makes the Batman and Robin story so special. While they were off fighting crime, the dynamic duo had Alfred back in the Batcave, making sure that they were well equipped with all the gadgets they needed to succeed in their mission, and that they had a safe and warm place to come home to after they defeated (or got beat up by) the bad folks.

When we talk about best friends at work, first we ask, how do you show up as an ally for yourself, by yourself? And then if you don't have your Robin or your Alfred yet, how do you actively reach out to others to build deep, one-to-one connections with those on your team? We ask these questions because that's how you deliver results and become allies for others.

Do you have at least one best friend at work—someone you trust, someone who has your back and you've got theirs, someone who challenges you to do more, to be more? If you do, then according to Gallup, you and your organization are at a definite advantage. But it's taken most businesses—and the people who run them—some time to wake up to this realization.

From Disconnection to Disengagement

If relationships matter (and they do—just ask your spouse or partner), then they matter even more at work. Most of us spend forty-plus hours a week alongside our colleagues, some of us many more (and research indicates that we have increased our hours in response to the pandemic). Add to that the time spent commuting to and from the office (or the bed-desk-bed commute when working from home), and it's easy to see why our work relationships often dominate *all* our relationships. It's not too far off to say that we spend roughly one-third of our time sleeping, one-third at work, and one-third doing all the other things we do. No surprise then that some of us have work relationships so strong and so deep that we describe the other person as a "work spouse."

You know you have strong professional relationships when you have people you can reach out to with questions when you are unsure of what action to take; these are winning relationships that empower you to achieve outstanding results together, the "I couldn't get my job done without you" relationships.

There's no doubt that the success you achieve ultimately depends on the quality of your professional relationships at work. Without effective relationships (you do have them, right?), your success will likely be compromised. When your people feel disconnected from their coworkers, their teams, and their bosses, they become disengaged from the company, their jobs, and their work. They will feel overworked, overwhelmed, overstressed, and undervalued. They may decide to get on board the train of the Great Resignation (the pandemic-spurred trend of many people quitting their jobs for better pay, better working conditions, or other reasons).

This is a big problem for organizations of all kinds in all places today. Fortunately, there is a solution: reinventing a sense of connection in a disconnected world.

Many years ago, Gallup started conducting research on employee engagement—defined by the company as employees "who are involved in, enthusiastic about, and committed to their work and workplace." The more employee engagement your organization has, the better the business outcomes. That was a significant finding, but even more important to Gallup was figuring out how the employee engagement needle could be moved upward.

During its research, Gallup tested and refined thousands of survey questions to determine which ones had the strongest links to employee engagement. The company labeled the result Q12—a set of twelve questions (surprise!) released in 1996 that "consistently and powerfully link to business outcomes, including profitability, employee retention, productivity, safety records, and customer engagement." In the years since, many millions of employees and teams around the globe have taken the Q12 survey.

Rather than bore you to tears with a dissertation on all twelve questions, we're going to focus on just one of them, the one that happens to pertain to the topic of this book—the infamous (and controversial) Q10:

Do you have a best friend at work?

Infamous? Controversial?

Yes, it's true. When Gallup introduced its Q12 survey more than two decades ago, many managers thought that this best friend question was far too touchy-feely to have any use in a business context. This was at a time when many business leaders practiced the belief that an employee's work and personal life should be rigidly divided—never the twain shall meet. As Gallup's Rodd Wagner and Jim Harter explained, "Invariably, one of the business leaders asks, 'Why do you ask that "best friend" question?' Sometimes their tone of voice communicates real curiosity. Sometimes it carries a tone of derision. Physicians bristle at it; it offends their clinical perspective. Attorneys scoff; 'irrelevant,' they object. Accountants consider it too far removed from the financial statements."

According to Wagner and Harter, the group of people most skeptical of the best friend question was executives. "One company cancelled a 12 Elements survey," they explained, "because it had just sent out a memo discouraging friendships. Others asked if the survey could be administered with just 11 of the 12 statements." Despite this initial resistance to the best friend question, Gallup defended it vigorously, and Q10 remains a vital part of the Q12 survey today.

Why?

Because having a best friend at work really matters. Gallup explains that "when employees have a deep sense of affiliation with their team members, they take positive actions that benefit the business—actions they may not otherwise even consider. Obviously, managers cannot manufacture friendships, but they can create situations for people to get to know each other and socialize without disrupting performance outcomes."

Perhaps it's no surprise that Gallup didn't just talk about the question, it also ran the numbers. And the numbers are

The success you
achieve ultimately depends
on the quality of your
professional relationships.

impressive. According to Gallup, employees who report having a best friend at work are:

- 43 percent more likely to report having received praise or recognition for their work in the last seven days

- 37 percent more likely to report that someone at work encourages their development

- 35 percent more likely to report coworker commitment to quality

- 28 percent more likely to report that, in the last six months, someone at work has talked to them about their progress

- 27 percent more likely to report that the mission of their company makes them feel their job is important

While we are big fans of Gallup and Q10 (do you have a best friend at work?) we have seen for ourselves, time and time again, that this only gets us part of the way to where we want to go as engaged, high-performing, and truly fabulous leaders. It's just one side of a coin that, like every other coin in the world, actually has *two* sides.

We believe that, despite the utter awesomeness of Q10, Gallup misses the mark when it comes to the most important part of the best friend equation. Here's the question each and every one of us should check ourselves on, every day of the week:

Am *I* a best friend at work?

While this might seem to be a subtle difference from Gallup's Q10, it comes from an entirely different place. Gallup's Q10 is *passive*: it only asks whether you have a best friend at work. Maybe you do, maybe you don't. That's cool.

The thing is, that's just not good enough—not by a long shot. You can't afford to passively wait for others to reach out to you to spark friendships at work that may or may not ever happen. That's putting all the many benefits of Gallup's Q10 to chance.

The *only* way you can ensure that you have a best friend at work is to *be* a best friend at work—to actively seek out, establish, build, and nurture these deep and long-lasting relationships with the people with whom you work. So, in the chapters that follow, we're going to constantly push the importance of actively being a best friend at work, not just to one other person (although that's a start) but to all your clients, colleagues, and vendors. And not just twiddling your thumbs, waiting for these critically important relationships to develop on their own, assuming they ever do. As workplace expert Dave Ulrich reminds us, "Work colleagues matter, work friends matter more, and friends who care about you outside of work may matter most."

If You Want to Go Far, Go Together

Aside from all the many benefits Gallup found in its research, there's another important reason for having a best friend at work: to counter the epidemic of loneliness, which is getting worse, not better. According to a survey of loneliness in the workplace conducted by Cigna in 2018, 54 percent of those surveyed reported feeling lonely. When Cigna conducted another survey of loneliness just one year later, that number had skyrocketed to 61 percent—seven percentage points. Imagine how that number has been negatively impacted because of the COVID-19 pandemic, which cut off many people from their usual work relationships. Loneliness at work is likely much worse than ever.

This very personal problem has a very real impact on organizations. Research shows that lonely workers are less engaged and less productive; they miss more days of work; the quality of their work is lower; and they have a higher turn-over rate.

And it only takes *one* friend at work to turn that tide around, according to research by Hakan Ozcelik and Sigal Barsade. People who are open to initiating, building, and maintaining meaningful friendships at work make an impression on those around them—that they *matter*. People are attracted to them; they care about them; they want to be their *allies*. Consider this example from Morag's personal experience:

I grew up in a traditional dad, mum, and two kids kind of family in East Anglia, England, though we moved a few times. My dad was the breadwinner, and my mum a part-time music teacher. Dad worked for the electricity board and was responsible for the distribution of electricity from big power generators across the network to various substations. Our typical holiday photos were "Ooh look—transmission cables! Switching gear!"

My dad was killed by an aortic aneurysm at the relatively young age of sixty-seven. He literally dropped down dead—no doubt as miffed about it as we were. As my brother shared in his eulogy, "Dad was invariably late for everything—on this occasion, we all agree, he was early." His funeral was a remarkable scene. It was standing room only, including an elementary school chum of my dad's from sixty years earlier who even brought along his own mother to the funeral. I don't recall my dad ever speaking negatively about others; he was generous with his time and attention. This was reflected in the powerful stories everyone shared during the funeral about how my dad had helped them and impacted their lives and careers in some way.

Growing up, when I moved in my own career—it didn't matter what I did or where I went—my dad always knew somebody. I remember one trip to the garden center, I'd moved a hundred miles down the road, and we bumped into somebody he knew. I remember thinking to myself, "Oh for heaven's sake, can't I do anything first? Has he been everywhere? Done everything? Know everyone?"

The irony is that this is now me. I'm the one who keeps bumping into people I know—work colleagues, people I've met as a result of a program I have facilitated or a keynote I have delivered. Forget the six degrees of separation; my belief is that, especially with technology, it's more like two degrees of connection. (You'll learn more about this idea later in the book.)

Work has always been fun to me. It doesn't matter what role I am fulfilling—whether a waitress, a banker, or now an entrepreneur—it has always been about the team. I remember not wanting to take part in office politics and backstabbing early in my career, because I didn't understand why we were fighting. We were all working for the same brand, the same company. "Why are we infighting?" I thought. "This is stupid." If you came and asked me for help, I would always do anything to help you. My belief has always been one of abundance: if you succeed, then we all succeed. As a keen sailor, the adage "a rising tide raises all boats" seems apt, versus the typical office politics which are more akin to scuttling the boat!

With hindsight, my dad was the inspiration and role model for my being an ally. However, back in the early days of my career, my thoughts on and concept of allies—and being an ally—in the workplace were still developing. I wasn't consistent in nurturing my ally relationships, especially as I progressed through my career. When I moved on to the next branch, the next job, I built my new network and didn't always stay connected with the old network. Only years later did I understand the importance of being and having best friends at work, and maintaining those close relationships—past, present, and into the future. Our success at SkyeTeam is a direct result of the quality of the relationships in our network. Thanks, Dad!

There's a South African word that packs a big message into just a small handful of letters (three of which just happen to be *u*). While *ubuntu* means *humanity* in the Nguni language, it has also been defined in terms of a Nguni proverb: "a person is a person through other people." In other words, none of us is an island—we accomplish more *together* than we do as individuals.

In a business context, ubuntu lends credence to the idea that if you want to go fast, go alone. But if you want to go far, *go together*.

However, that's easier said than done for those who think that *me* first instead of *we* first is where it's at. Although schools have been slowly changing their emphasis from individual student performance to team performance, many of us grew up in an environment where independence and individualism were routinely taught and rewarded. (We'll assume for now that you weren't a student at Hogwarts learning how to make charms and potions and fly on broomsticks.) It was *me* versus that pop quiz sitting on top of my desk. *Me* versus my teacher, who was always trying to prove to the class that I hadn't studied. *Me* versus my classmates—especially that bully who kept trying to take my lunch money.

And what happened if you "collaborated" with a classmate on a test—sharing the wealth of your intellectual prowess by providing them with your answers? Chances are, if you were caught by your teacher, this tremendous act of teamwork earned you an immediate trip to the principal's office; an F on the test; and a nasty note for your parents to read, sign, and promptly return (getting you grounded for a week or more).

Truth be told, it doesn't matter if you're serving up burgers in a fast-food restaurant, running a high-powered consulting firm, or part of a 100,000-person global manufacturing organization, it's all about the *team*. Sure, you still have to be personally good at what you do—you have to know your stuff—but your success increasingly depends on your ability to work with a team, leveraging each member's individual talents. Even solopreneurs depend on others to get their work done. Teamwork makes the dream work, right?

But this emphasis on teamwork and collaboration is not something that many managers take time to explain or work through with their new employees. They're just thrown into the deep end of the pool without so much as a rainbow unicorn floaty. It's sink or swim, shark eat shark, and survival of the fittest. Sadly, far too many employees end up sinking instead of swimming, or they become chum for those hungry sharks that regularly consume newbies as a tasty breakfast treat.

What's needed is a framework—a road map—that describes how we relate to others in the workplace and shows us how we can move from less effective to more effective behavior patterns. How we can be a best friend at work? The Relationship Ecosystem, our approach to describing how to relate to others on the job, provides that framework—and much more.

You, me, we—
the relationship
superpower we
all need.

The Relationship Ecosystem

The Relationship Ecosystem (a concept introduced by Morag in *Cultivate*) brings the human back into the workplace—breaking down the politics, silos, and turf wars that ultimately slow down information, degrade decision quality, and get in the way of business success. The Relationship Ecosystem is a way of thinking about who you are dependent on for your success—your boss, team, peers, industry experts, and so on—and how you would describe the health of your relationship. The health of your relationship can range from "Ugh, she's a jerk—I'll never have her on my team" to "I would love to work with her anytime."

Let's have a closer look.

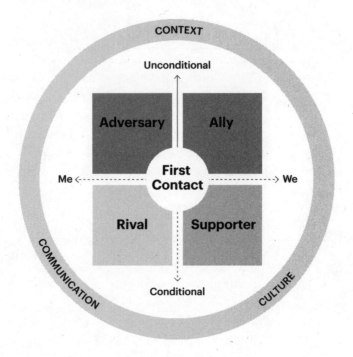

As you can see, there are both outer and inner parts to the model. The outer part—the macro or fifty-thousand-foot level—focuses on three areas:

- The context of your relationships—the current expectations placed on the relationships by the roles you hold in the organization, along with the history and baggage that comes with preexisting relationships

- The organizational culture in which your relationships occur

- The communication used to describe the relationship—both the communication style of each individual and the conversation you will need to have to move the relationship forward

It's in the inner part of the model, however, where the real action takes place. This is the intrapersonal micro level where you build (and destroy) relationships with others, whether as individuals or teams, from the very first contact to today.

There are two axes: the *me to we* axis (horizontal) and the *conditional to unconditional* axis (vertical).

The *me* end of the horizontal axis is where you are focused 100 percent on yourself to the exclusion of others. Raging narcissists live here, but rarely anyone else. The *we* end of the horizontal axis is where you're focused 100 percent on the group, including yourself but not putting yourself above others. Again, relatively few people are 100 percent *we* focused—most people do look out for number one from time to time, and that's to be expected. After all, you've got to toot your own horn sometimes to get noticed; you have to say no to others so you can say yes to yourself and your needs. It's about balance.

The vertical axis—*conditional to unconditional*—is where you determine just how committed you are to act in a certain way. When a relationship is *conditional*, this means you act only in ways that are in your interest to do so at that moment in time. You assess the situation to decide, for example, whether to lend another person your support or work against them in a given situation. When a relationship is *unconditional*, however, you are always going to act in a certain way—having weighed the pros and cons first and acting accordingly. This can be a good thing when you are willing to lend your support with a *we* mindset whenever you need it. Or it can be a bad thing when you adopt the *me* mindset and decide to constantly challenge or fight every decision.

We're going to guess that by now you've noticed that these two axes create four quadrants. We call these quadrants the *four relationship dynamics*, and they determine the exact nature of the relationships you form with others—both at work and in your personal life. Let's consider each in turn.

Adversary

While it might seem that we are splitting hairs when we talk about adversaries versus rivals, there *is* a difference. With an adversary, you're always looking over your shoulder to make sure they're not about to stab you in the back, and they might do it overtly (out in the open) or covertly (undercover). It's all about *me* for adversaries, and the relationship is unconditional in nature: you can always count on them to challenge you. The adversary's motto is "I am against you!"

Rival

We all know what it feels like to have a rival: someone who may be competing with us for resources and rewards. It's all about *me*—some of the time—and the relationships rivals form with others are conditional. That is, they may choose to support you or not depending on what's in it for *them*. It can feel like you are working with both Jekyll and Hyde. The rival's motto is "I am ahead of you."

Supporter

It's definitely a good thing to have people in your work and personal life who are supporters. They are focused on *we*—they cheer you on, and they can be relied on to help you when times are good. However, since relationships with them are conditional, they tend to be fair-weather friends. They're not willing to stick their necks out for you or for others. When times get tough, their support may suddenly evaporate—leaving you in the lurch. The supporter's motto is "I'm right behind you."

Ally

An ally is the best of both worlds: they are focused on *we* instead of *me*, and they provide their support unconditionally, in good times and in bad. Allies always have your back; they provide you with frank and honest feedback; and they are invested in your success—just as you are likely invested in *their* success. The ally's motto is "I'm right here with you."

Allies typically have these characteristics:

- They have your back, always
- They share a common interest or goal with you
- They work to achieve the same results
- They share their experience and provide coaching
- They act as a sounding board for your ideas
- They tell you what you need, not just want, to hear
- They are with you on the good days and especially on the bad ones

Think for a moment about the popular Disney film *The Lion King*, which beautifully illustrates the nature of ally relationships. Simba's Relationship Ecosystem looked something like this: Scar was Simba's pure adversary—he wanted Simba dead so *he* could be king. The hyenas were rivals—not direct adversaries but supporters of Scar. Most of the other lions were supporters of Simba, while Timon and Pumbaa were his allies; they were willing to put themselves at great personal risk to ensure he became the rightful king. They were right there with Simba, every step of the way.

We are convinced that having an ally is the pinnacle of relationships. Your allies are your best friends at work, and in turn, you are best friends at work to your allies. Just to be clear, we're not talking about having one single best friend. We're talking about having a mindset where you are a best friend to all.

Remember, it goes both ways, and you may need to make the first move. In fact, true best friends at work take an active role in reaching out to others to spark relationships and build deep connections. You find a way to meet each other where you're at, and you stick with each other through thick and thin—through the good times and the bad.

The best relationships stand the test of time. They *endure*.

The True Test

How do you show up as an ally—as a best friend at work? It's easy to be an ally when things are going well, when everyone is getting their bonuses and the sales are coming in. And with people you like, it's also easy.

The true relationship test is in the tough times—like the year 2020, which careened off the road and exploded in the ditch in a spectacular way—especially with the people who grate on you and you clash with. You don't want to be drawn down to their level and become a rival. Nor do you want to become passive and think, "Well, because you suck and I don't like working with you, I'm not going to tell you why that'll never work," but never articulate it. You need to find a way to step into your truth and muster the courage to share those tough messages—to give warnings of impending disaster because it's the right thing to do for everyone.

That way is something we call the Ally Mindset.

The Ally Mindset connects to your personal values. It connects to your personal brand. And it connects deeply to your emotions. As the saying goes, people may forget what you said or did, but they will never forget how you made them feel. Developing your Ally Mindset is what moves your focus from me to we. It's what inspires you to consider the other *you* in the equation—what their hopes, needs, desires might be— and empowers you to share your own personal hopes, needs, and desires to work toward mutual success.

You, me, we—the relationship superpower we all need.

That's what it means to be an ally. With an ally, what you see is what you get. There are no hidden agendas.

Of course, being an ally isn't always easy. In fact, it can be hard work to build and maintain ally relationships. However, like many other things that aren't easy, being an ally is worthwhile—there's real value in it for you and for the people in your work and personal life.

In the next chapter, we take a detailed look at the Ally Mindset—what it is, the essential practices that enable it, and how to make the Ally Mindset work for you in your professional and personal life.

THE ALLY MINDSET

We're All
#BetterTogether

66

They may forget what you said—
but they will never forget
how you made them feel.

CARL W. BUEHNER

WHEN MORAG sat down with this particular leader—a senior director in an up-and-coming tech startup—on that particular day, to say he was in a sorry state of shame and disappointment with himself would be a tremendous understatement. He was pacing back and forth in the office, frustrated with his team, and angry at his boss for the not so delicately delivered feedback that he had just received. For a moment, Morag could have sworn she saw trails of smoke streaming from the leader's ears, like a furious character in some children's cartoon.

"Eff this" and "Eff that," Biff (his alias for the purpose of today) muttered under his breath as he continued to pace, occasionally punching the air with his closed fist for emphasis.

Morag, serving as his executive coach, sat quietly in a chair next to Biff's desk as his rage continued to build. Her thoughts were going a million miles an hour: there must be some way to defuse this thermonuclear warhead before he self-detonated, potentially obliterating everyone in his presence. The stress levels were palpable, apoplexy personified, and it was starting to cause Morag's own heart rate to increase.

She decided that the best strategy would be to sit back and wait. He was certain to calm down at some point, right?

Sure enough, like an exhausted puppy after an extended session of chasing its tail, Biff slowed his pacing and his bright-red face began to return to its normal color. He sat down at his desk and let out a deep sigh.

That's when Morag made her move.

She explored what had set him off and why he was so upset.

It quickly came out that Biff had delivered a message to his team in his usual style, and it had fallen flat—he had not stuck the landing. Perhaps worst of all, at least in his mind, Biff had not won the undying admiration and thanks of his team for (what seemed to him) a logical decision and call to action. And it's no wonder. As some of Biff's direct reports described to Morag afterward, their boss was a triple-A leader: an arrogant, aggressive asshole.

When his team hadn't rushed to adopt the new process he had outlined, and instead resisted his message, Biff didn't step back, take stock of the situation, and regroup; he completely lost control. He barked out defenses, meted out punishments he would never enforce, and said far too many personally offensive things he now regretted. And that's when his boss called him with the not-so-delicate feedback of "Get your shit together and lead your team!" (Yes, we recognize another triple-A leader in action, but that's a story for another time and another book!)

When Morag dug deeper with the members of Biff's team, she discovered that this was not the first time they had described him as a triple-A leader, and that his team felt unheard because he was so blunt and direct in his communication style. From his perspective, he was just speaking his truth. The irony was that everything he was sharing about where the business needed to go was 100 percent right. But the people on his team didn't care because they didn't feel included in the process—and they weren't.

Mark Manson is the author of one of our favorite books, *The Subtle Art of Not Giving a F*ck*. He offers a small bit of advice that really resonates with us: "When in doubt, check your intentions." The further Morag and Biff explored what had triggered his rage, it came down to one simple thing: he had not invested in building connected and compassionate relationships with his people, and as a result his intent had been misunderstood by them.

In the research we conducted for this book, we found that 67 percent of people reported that their success has been undermined by the words or actions of their colleagues. Think about that for a moment: 67 percent of regular people working in everyday workplaces—small businesses, large multinationals, and everything in between. That's a significant portion of us, no matter what our job is or where or for whom we work.

In fact, if your success isn't being undermined by others in the organization, then chances are you may very well be busy undermining or sabotaging the success of someone else—either intentionally as a rival or adversary or unintentionally as a supporter. And that's exactly what was happening with the senior director who was sitting in front of Morag. He was *brilliant*, but he was a *brilliant jerk*. He constantly pointed his finger at others, assigning blame for every team and organizational failure to everyone but himself.

It's no coincidence that nearly two-thirds of American employees report that, at one time or another, they have worked in a toxic workplace. And it's probably no surprise to most of us that more than one-fourth of these employees report they have worked in *more* than one toxic workplace. All this bad behavior results in all sorts of negative outcomes, including hurt feelings, stress, employee disengagement, and lost productivity.

The Ally Mindset
is an intentional, conscious
choice to be proactive
and thoughtful in your
relationships rather
than reactive and defensive
in your interactions.

And when that jerk is the boss? Things can get even worse. Gallup found that bad bosses are the number one reason why people quit their jobs. And McKinsey reports that 56 percent of workers would describe their boss as mildly or highly toxic, with 75 percent indicating that interacting with their boss is the most stressful part of their workday. While some of your good people might stick around for years in a negative environment that makes them feel like you-know-what on a stick—putting up with a toxic boss or jerk-o-rific coworkers because of deep loyalty or love of the mission—many of your best people have likely already left, finding much greener grass on the other side of the proverbial fence.

Morag didn't want this to be Biff's ultimate legacy, and thankfully neither did he. And neither did the company's leadership, who supported Biff by providing an executive coach. Everyone wanted Biff to do better—*be* better—and the first step would be improving his relationships at work. (Who knows? Maybe he could also avoid an expensive divorce or a night in the doghouse by improving his relationships at *home* too!)

As Morag began to work with Biff, she explained to him that while we can't always control what happens to us, we *can* control how we interpret what happens to us and how we choose to respond. When the leader calmed down and looked at the two sides of the equation, he could see where the disconnect had happened. His epiphany was that his "misunderstood genius" act was being classified as being a "brilliant jerk" by others, and he was not responding well to the new knowledge. If he was going to build better relationships with his people, he had to stop pointing fingers and ascribing blame. He needed to look inward, to go first in changing how he showed up.

He was actively undermining the people who worked for and with him, but he wasn't doing it on purpose—that was never his intent. His default was simply getting directly to the point without drawing on the opinions or input or assistance of others. And so he trained his people to withhold opinions, input, and assistance. Sometimes, through action or inaction, or through conversations you have or don't have, you create the very outcomes you are trying so hard to avoid.

How often have you undermined others—intentionally or unintentionally? How often have you railed against others and caused them to withdraw, disengage from their work, or even quit their jobs? How often have you burned your bridges of trust with the very people on whom you depend for the success of your team and your organization—and yourself?

As it turned out, Biff had his own share of problems. Morag discovered in her discussions with Biff that he wasn't enjoying work at all; he knew his job would be at risk if he couldn't reconnect with his team and build positive, strong relationships. Because of Biff's leadership style, his team wasn't delivering, and so he found himself burning the candle at both ends. He felt like he was working around the clock and the proverbial eight days a week. This stress and overwork was bleeding into his personal life; his family was mad at him too because they weren't getting Biff's presence and focus. He was always thinking about work, doing work, being caught up in work.

In her coaching, Morag and Biff together identified how he could dial down his negative behaviors at work and dial up his positive ones. He began starting meetings and one-on-ones with a more personal question that built connection instead of disabling it: "*How* are you doing?" versus "*What* are you doing?" For just a minute or two to break the ice, he also shared a little of what he was thinking and feeling. He opened up and showed a more humane and human leadership style—his Ally Mindset.

Biff asked his people questions instead of imposing his own views or demanding that others listen to his perspective. He paused before answering, whether that was answering his own questions or answering questions from others. That pause modeled "I heard you; let me think about what I heard." He was very clear on service level agreements (SLAs) for the team regarding availability and responsiveness on Slack and other platforms. He introduced the weekly habit of gratitude—giving recognition and saying thank you to his people. And he started saying no to things that weren't aligned with the team's priorities.

Within six months, the relationships between this leader and the members of his team had completely turned around. His team finally felt empowered and valued, and they routinely stepped up and were having fun at work!

Biff also turned his attention to his personal life. He started working out again—running three times a week and looking after his personal health and wellness. He set some new ground rules at home: no working on the weekends (well, at least not on Saturdays), no phones at mealtimes (he would be fully present), date nights with his spouse, and family nights with everyone. His relationships with his spouse and the members of his family improved and deepened dramatically.

The apoplectic outbursts in the office were gone, ghosts of Biff's past. As they completed their coaching program, Biff shared with Morag that he felt lighter at work—that he was having fun again. He's no longer a triple-A leader—he's now a leader that people want to work for and with. He lost fifteen pounds, and his family unit is stronger and happier. It was a 180-degree turn in both his work life and personal life.

If you want to build your network of close friends at work (and by now, we hope you see the wisdom in doing so), then you have to do one very important thing: adopt an Ally

Mindset. The Ally Mindset is all about forging the human connection, and it is the first step in building stronger relationships on the job by creating allies—people whom you can count on, whom you can depend on, who care about you, and who trust you. It's all about how you show up and how others feel in your presence—and also when you're not in the room with them.

In making choices about how we show up in our relationships, Ruby uses the phrase *deep presence*. Being present is one thing, but deep presence is an entirely different level of connection with another person. It's an intentional choice to pour energy into being there in that moment. When we talk with our clients or one another, we make a point of listening intently to what the other person is saying, not only for the details of the story but also for what's going on underneath the surface. How they truly feel about things, which frames what we ask next.

This requires turning off our problem-solving mind. We can offer solutions, but the other person may not have the same view as we do. They don't have the same internal and external resources we have; they don't have the same life experiences; they don't have the same levels of vulnerability or courage; and on and on. We're all different, and we have to meet people where they are—not try to bring them to where we are. Like snowflakes, no two of us are identically alike, and we must keep that in mind as we reach out to help and support others.

The simple truth: you can't be a success in business and life if your interpersonal relationships are broken. McKinsey analysis revealed that 25 percent of our life satisfaction comes from the satisfaction we feel with our job. And 39 percent of our job satisfaction comes from the interpersonal relationships we have at work—particularly relationships we have with our boss and other managers.

How would you grade the quality of your work relationships? Great? Okay? Not so great? Can't-wait-to-quit-this-stinking-job bad? It's okay—you can tell us. We won't tell anyone.

The Ally Mindset propels us forward. It aligns with our personal values. It allows us to be at our best when circumstances or others might be encouraging us to be at our worst. And when we're at our best, we help others to be at *their* best.

It's All about Allies

While we have always needed allies in our work and life, this is especially the case today. It's no secret that we have endured one of the most difficult situations for humankind in many decades. The COVID-19 pandemic tore many of us out of our workplaces and squirreled us away in our homes where we had to figure out how to get our work done. We thought it would be over in a matter of weeks, and instead it dragged on for years.

For many of us, this meant canceling meetings, business travel, and attendance at conferences and symposiums; working from home as we created impromptu offices in spare bedrooms, dining rooms, or even closets; being forced literally overnight to become in-home Zoom teachers for our kids, who were prohibited from attending school in person; and simultaneously juggling all the usual commitments with family, friends, and neighbors. And for no small number of us, it meant being laid off, furloughed, or fired—wondering where the next paycheck was going to come from.

In a time when intentionally reaching out to others to build relationships was even more important, we had less energy and capacity to do so. During this difficult period, our relationship muscles atrophied, and we unlearned how to connect with others and build community and commitment.

We lost the knack for making small talk, and it will take more than a shot in the arm to rejuvenate the relationships we've neglected. We're learning how to coexist with COVID-19, and many workplaces will continue in some sort of hybrid mode— partly in person at the office, and partly remote, connecting with our coworkers, customers, and others via email, Zoom, Slack, and other digital communications platforms.

This new reality of the workplace makes the relationship skills we present in the chapters that follow critically import- ant for your ongoing success. Are you ready to get going? Now is the time to be deliberate, thoughtful, and proactive in how you rekindle your connections and in how you show up in your relationships at work (and at home). Let's take a closer look at the Ally Mindset—what it is and how it can bring about a positive change in your leadership and in your life.

The Ally Mindset

The *Merriam-Webster* definitions of *mindset* are "a mental atti- tude or inclination" and "a fixed state of mind." We would take these definitions a step further and define *mindset* as a perspective that we carry, or a lens we look through, as we approach the world around us. Our lens or perspective defines our words, actions, how we approach situations, the choices we make, and how we view life's challenges. In short, our mindset exerts a tremendous amount of influence over our behavior, both in and out of the workplace.

To be honest, we're not raving fans of *Merriam-Webster*'s second definition above, particularly as it relates to the Ally Mindset. The kind of mindset we're talking about is a series of choices that we constantly make, in real time; it's the filter we look through to perceive the world around us. It defines the choices and opportunities (or lack thereof) that we see laid out

The Ally Mindset
is all about forging the
human connection.

in front of us. It's a bit like a board game—think chess, Monopoly, or even Candy Land. Where you are located on the board defines the possible paths ahead and the choices and options you see laid out in front of you, like the chess pieces zipping across the ceiling—upside down—in *The Queen's Gambit*.

There will be times, for example, when you'll want to be more direct with others and shout your message from the rooftops to make sure everyone hears and understands it. And there will be times when you'll want to deliberately turn down the volume, go into active listening mode, and approach the conversation with curiosity. You need to first know the goal you're trying to achieve, then you need to be mindful of your default reactions so you can be intentional about how you show up for others.

The Ally Mindset is an intentional, conscious choice to be proactive and thoughtful in your relationships rather than reactive and defensive in your interactions. It is a perspective you hold that defines your presence as a leader, how others *feel* in your presence, and how *you* feel in your *own* presence (especially if you are lying awake worrying about work at one o'clock in the morning). It's adopting a *we* instead of *me* mindset where *we all win together*.

Emotions drive behavior, especially when you are unaware of them. When negative emotions or self-talk are driving behavior, this can lead to a reactive mindset. When you are stressed, under pressure, worried, and so on (like Biff from earlier), you will feel limited in your choices and maybe backed into a corner. This can lead to a *me* mindset, where you might not be able to see beyond the current moment. Your world becomes very small.

When you carry a *we* mindset, you think beyond yourself. You know that you are not alone, and you see lots of options. This is not a mirage, not your imagination—there really *are* more options available to you when you think beyond your-self. You open the floodgates of possibility when you tap into the great ideas, skills, and talents of others and invite them to join you on your own journey. The *we* mindset includes an understanding of *you*, your perspective, and your wants and needs. It encompasses the *me*, my perspective, my wants and needs, and it creates a shared understanding and way forward that respects us both. Better together.

Taking on a proactive Ally Mindset requires self-awareness. What is driving your behavior? What is your starting point? What mindset is shaping your choices? You have to recognize your own stories. The Ally Mindset also requires letting go of what you think others should do. Regardless of what you get back from others, you consciously and intentionally choose to stay in an Ally Mindset. Yes, there will be good days and bad days, but it is about choosing this even when, and especially when, work and life get difficult.

When you adopt the Ally Mindset and build a strong net-work of best friends at work, you'll do more than build your relationships, you'll create the conditions necessary for the three Cs to take root and flourish.

Community because success is a team sport.

Commitment as you prepare to take on your greatest goals.

Connection when you realize you'll never have to feel alone at work again.

The Ally Mindset is your baseline, your grounding, the keel on the sailboat of your life. The five practices of the Ally Mind-set provide a framework for intentional choices in all your relationships. Which lines do you need to tighten or loosen to change the nature of a relationship at a specific time? What circumstances or challenges that pop up in everyday life require you to take a different tack? How do you set your sails? If you've ever found yourself trapped in the doldrums because of your own choices, or needed a safe path out, you're in the right place.

So, what are the essential practices of the Ally Mindset— the building blocks that give it so much power? We thought you'd never ask.

The Five Practices of the Ally Mindset

If you want to build your network of close friends at work (and the research we presented above shows why you should), then you've got to do one very important thing: adopt an Ally Mindset. The five practices of the Ally Mindset emerged from our research, the data from the Ally Mindset Profile, and the insights from leaders and participants in our many programs. The following practices are further developed in later chapters.

Abundance and Generosity

This practice is all about working with others—about *being* rather than *doing*—and it is the first step in moving from a *me-first* to a *we-first* orientation. Having an Ally Mindset begins with having a perspective of *abundance*: you believe there's plenty of success to go around and that collaborating for the success of others in your workplace and network will create more success for everyone. While abundance is a good start, it needs to be coupled with *generosity* to deliver the full impact. For leaders, this means coaching, mentoring, and sharing your experiences with those who work for you and with you to ensure you all succeed together. In chapter 3, we'll dive deep into this practice and discover how it can help you achieve an Ally Mindset.

Connection and Compassion

It's no secret that we humans are hardwired for *connection* with one another; it's built into our DNA and reinforced with every positive relationship we enjoy during the course of our lives. Building an Ally Mindset requires really connecting with people in the workplace, including coworkers, customers, vendors, and even your boss. But it requires more than connection. It also requires *compassion*—having empathy for the highs and lows of those you connect with and being able to put yourself in their shoes. You cheer their successes and mourn their losses. You practice *radical humanity*, assuming positive intent on the part of others and putting people before profits. In chapter 4, we'll show you how to use connection and compassion to build stronger relationships with others.

Courage and Vulnerability

Key to developing an Ally Mindset is having the ability to reveal yourself completely to others, warts and all. This

The simple truth is this:
you can't be a success
in business and life if
your interpersonal
relationships are broken.

requires the *courage* to admit to your shortcomings and mistakes and being open to feedback. It also requires demonstrating *vulnerability*—owning up to your fears or concerns, asking others for help, and acting on that help when it is provided. Once you have forged a connection with others, you can be courageous and vulnerable. While some think that vulnerability is a weakness, it's really a strength that can help us build relationships with others. In chapter 5, we'll explore how courage and vulnerability work together in the Ally Mindset.

Candor and Debate

As every leader knows, effective communication is critically important to the success of any team or organization. This means having the right conversations at the right time and ensuring that these conversations are completely honest and transparent. This also means being an active listener and fully participating in these conversations. *Candor* is the ability to share your point of view in a way that increases learning and shared understanding, and it also means providing and receiving tough feedback. *Debate* is the willingness to take a stand and then defend it in discussions with others—often passionately, but always respectfully. Cultivating allies is about discussing the undiscussables before they become barriers. Together, candor and debate can resolve conflict and help solve difficult business problems—by converting them into opportunities. In chapter 6, we'll take a close look at the practice of candor and debate and explain how you can use it to your advantage.

Action and Accountability

Action is doing something, and in the context of the Ally Mindset, it is reactive in nature. It's doing what you say you're going to do when you say you'll do it. *Accountability* is looking out for the needs of others proactively; that is, you think about what they need to be successful. It's seeing what's going on around you and helping others. It's about the choices you make and how you show up in each of your relationships— *doing* behaviors consistently, especially when having difficult conversations or in times of uncertainty. And it's about acting on and being accountable to the four other components of the Ally Mindset. If, for example, you have abundance and generosity but never do anything with those qualities, you won't end up where you want to go. In chapter 7, we'll consider how to build an Ally Mindset with this essential practice.

When you adopt an Ally Mindset, you're presented with a golden opportunity to...

Increase your self-awareness and amplify your leadership presence. Ask yourself, Which practices am I overusing or underusing? Which ones come more naturally to me? You might, for example, be amazing at keeping your commitments (action and accountability), but you don't speak up for yourself when you are overloaded with work (courage and vulnerability).

Strengthen your relationships. Where might you need to turn the dial up or down on one of the practices to strengthen a relationship? For example, you might have one relationship where you especially struggle with speaking your truth. If that's the case, you know that you can strengthen your relationships by working on the practice of candor and debate.

Improve the performance of your team and organization. How do you demonstrate the Ally Mindset within your team? How are the five practices blocked or encouraged in your organization (for example, by processes, big changes, structure, lack of organizational learning, lack of focus, silos, and so on)? What might you want to shift to improve performance in your organization?

This endeavor is not about perfection every single day in all five of the practices. It's about always striving to do your best—to chip away at your negatives and incrementally do more of your positives. It's about understanding who you are at the core (me); your natural preferences, the context in which you are leading, and your relationships (you); and when and where to turn the dial up or down on each practice to ensure mutual success (we) by making an overt choice.

Here's an analogy: Morag is a classical musician. Assume we are friends and you've come to listen to Yo-Yo Ma perform Elgar's Cello Concerto with the Broomfield Symphony Orchestra (where Morag was the principal bassoonist). As you listen to the concert, sitting quietly (no humming allowed), and as the emotion of the final movement grows, you remain stoic. As the conductor lowers the baton (and not a moment before!), you provide genteel applause or maybe, because you love this piece so much, enthusiastic clapping. Meanwhile Morag is in the back row of the orchestra, quietly shedding a tear at the emotion and looking to see your reaction.

Now let's switch scenes. We're headed to see Eric and his band, Rogue 2, perform at a local brewpub. Here you don't sit quietly; in fact, you are expected to sing along, get up and dance, whoop with your applause, and let it all hang out. An overt display of teamwork, enthusiasm, and engagement.

You and I haven't changed who we are between the two venues; we're the same people. We have the same feelings, core values, and needs. What has changed is the context in which we are experiencing our relationship, demonstrating our leadership, and the expected behaviors appropriate for expressing appreciation and enjoyment.

Choosing the wrong behavior in the wrong location—for example, applauding between movements at the classical concert—will get you frowns and tuts. Singing along and dancing in the aisle during the performance will likely get you removed from the auditorium. Similarly, sitting quietly through Eric's gig is likely to convince everyone you aren't having fun, and potentially question your friendship.

Being an ally and nurturing your Ally Mindset—to thoughtfully and deliberately choose how you need to show up to ensure the best experience for all—helps all parties to be present before, during, and after each interaction. It starts with you, who you are, what you desire, and it encompasses me, my perspective, my life story. When we come together—when we focus on the you, me, and we—that's where the magic happens, and the multiplier effect kicks into high gear.

Make no mistake about it, improving your relationships with others is always going to be a work in progress. But it's a good work in progress—one that everyone should make a point of pursuing at every opportunity.

A Short Note about Allyship

At this point, we would like to take the opportunity to briefly address how this book connects to the idea of *allyship* in a diversity, equity, and inclusion (DE&I) context. While there are many definitions of *allyship* to be found out in the wild, here is the definition used by Nicole Asong Nfonoyim-Hara, the director of the diversity programs at Mayo Clinic:

> When a person of privilege works in solidarity and partnership with a marginalized group of people to help take down the systems that challenge that group's basic rights, equal access, and ability to thrive in our society.

In addition to the hardships of the global pandemic, the US came face to face with deep racial inequities and injustice in

2020. This movement has elevated the terms *ally* and *allyship*, which are important roles in moving away from racial injustice and toward true equity and inclusion.

In this context, demonstrating allyship or being an ally is a role that those with power and privilege take on to step up and speak out to remove barriers for those who do not have that same power and privilege. In this book, we speak of an *ally* as someone who demonstrates an "unconditional we" approach in relationships, in both personal and professional contexts. This means that in relationships: (1) you are focused on *our* mutual success (we) versus *my own* individual success (me), and (2) you show up consistently (unconditionally—in other words, what you see is what you get).

In the context of racial injustice, we are called to show up unconditionally for the benefit of us *all*. As such, these two concepts—demonstrating allyship and demonstrating an Ally Mindset—are very much aligned. Each of the Ally Mindset practices also apply to allyship: abundance and generosity, connection and compassion, courage and vulnerability, candor and debate, and action and accountability.

For example, if you are in a position of power and privilege, and it is your intention to step into an allyship role, you must demonstrate each of these five practices to do that well. To demonstrate allyship, you must be generous in your time and actions, deeply connect with those around you, be courageous enough to have the tough conversations, be willing to challenge the people and processes that get in the way of true equality, and ultimately act and keep your word.

So, although we are not explicitly laying out the concepts in this allyship arena, know that they 100 percent *do* apply to allyship and help to eliminate racial injustice one relationship at a time.

LOOK UP, SHOW UP, STEP UP

At the end of each chapter, we offer some actions you can take and ask some simple but profoundly powerful questions for you to reflect on. We challenge you to *look up*—and notice the relationship dynamic, consider how you feel, and understand how you want others to feel in your presence. You can then be intentional about how you need to *show up* for that relationship. Finally, you'll *step up*, which means you follow through and take the appropriate action. Here's the first set for you to consider.

- **Reflect and renew your Ally Mindset.** To grow your Ally Mindset, you need a language and framework to measure against. Take the Ally Mindset Profile at SkyeTeam.cloud/YouMeWe. Then regularly reflect on how consistently you role-model Ally Mindset behaviors. Which of the practices come easily to you? Which may require more thoughtful application?

- **Demonstrate an Ally Mindset—be a truth speaker and truth seeker.** Instead of focusing on the risk of speaking up, consider the risk of not speaking up. This simple reversal of risk assessment makes it more likely that you will speak up. Ask questions, share information, communicate consistently—learn to think out loud. Develop a reputation for straight talk, coupled with curiosity and learning, and others can follow your lead.

- **Admit your mistakes, and celebrate your beautiful failures.** Smart leaders know the tremendous power of admitting their mistakes; they show others that they are human while driving fear out of the organization. Morag heard a radio program about a Chinese theater production of the play *War Horse* (which was also adapted by Steven Spielberg). It took four people to operate the life-sized puppet horse in the play, requiring tremendous skill, coordination, and teamwork. In

the radio program, the host asked about the learning process including the mistakes, and the actors challenged that
phrase, instead reframing mistakes as "getting into a room
and making beautiful failures." To grow your Ally Mindset, turn
your human mistakes into beautiful failures, learn from them,
adjust your approach, and move on.

- **Being an ally is a team sport.** To have an ally/best friend at
work, you need to be an ally/best friend at work. As you start
to flex your Ally Mindset capabilities, enlist the support of your
colleagues and friends. Ask for feedback to help you improve
(the *me* focus) and then turn your attention to the needs of
those around you (the *we* focus).

Take some time to reflect on the following questions:

- How do you define what it means to be an ally? How consistently do you embody your own definition? What intentional
choices are you making with every conversation?

- Are you considering the three Cs in your relationships? Are you
intentionally choosing to build *community*? To explicitly state
your *commitment*? To make real *connections*?

- Like classical concerts and rock shows, are you making venue-
appropriate choices in each of your conversations?

- How might your colleagues describe your leadership reputation and impact? How closely is this aligned with the legacy
and reputation you aspire to?

3

ABUNDANCE AND GENEROSITY

Be the Flame That
Lights Another's Candle

66

That's what I consider true
generosity: you give your all and yet you
always feel as if it costs you nothing.

SIMONE DE BEAUVOIR

ABUNDANCE AND GENEROSITY are all about working with others, and they are the first step in moving from a *me-first* to a *we-first* orientation. An Ally Mindset begins with holding a perspective of *abundance*: you believe there's plenty of success to go around and that collaborating for the success of others in your workplace and network will create more success for *everyone*. A rising tide raises all boats, right? (So long as it's not a tsunami!)

It's what Simon Sinek describes as the *infinite mindset*—that the games of business and life today have no fixed rules, no clear end point, no beginning, no end, no winners, and no losers—just ahead and behind. This game is played for the purpose of continuing the play for as long as you possibly can, not for immediate gain.

In his book *The Infinite Game*, Sinek tells the story about how his experience with Apple, which he says had an infinite mindset, differed from Microsoft, which had a finite mindset—where business and life have fixed rules, a clear beginning and end, and are played for the sole purpose of winning. Says Sinek,

Some years ago, I spoke at an educational summit for Microsoft. A few months later, I spoke at an educational

summit for Apple. At the Microsoft event, the majority of
the presenters devoted a good portion of their presentations to talking about how they were going to beat Apple.
At the Apple event, 100 percent of the presenters spent
100 percent of their time talking about how Apple was
trying to help teachers teach and help students learn. One
group seemed obsessed with beating their competition.
The other group seemed obsessed with advancing a cause.

Which company would you rather work for? Which one do
you think would make you feel more fulfilled and result in
significantly fewer ulcers and bar visits after work over the
long haul?

Continues Sinek, "To ask, 'What's best for me' is finite
thinking. To ask, 'What's best for us' is infinite thinking. A
company built for the Infinite Game doesn't think of itself
alone. It considers the impact of its decisions on its people, its
community, the economy, the country, and the world." James
Carse, NYU's director of religious studies who originated the
concepts of finite and infinite games, writes, "The finite play
for life is serious; the infinite play of life is joyous."

While abundance is a good start (and yes, you do need
to get started *somewhere*), it must be coupled with *generosity*
to deliver the full impact. For leaders, this means coaching,
mentoring, and sharing your experiences—good, bad, and
indifferent—with those who work for and with you to help
ensure you all succeed together.

Mindsets are contagious—at least they are when you share
what you are thinking and what you believe, and then follow
through with living and demonstrating them every day. If you
are working in a toxic environment, if you are experiencing
rival or adversarial dog-eat-dog behaviors, if you want to create healthy competition and a strong team of allies, then you

need to nurture your Ally Mindset. This all starts with abundance and generosity.

As you can imagine, we have done far more workshops and keynote presentations on the Ally Mindset than we can remember. One thing we do remember, however, is that we have collected data from attendees along the way—asking them how they feel when abundance and generosity are strengths or are lacking in their workplaces.

When they are strengths, our attendees share these kinds of words to describe the feelings and dynamics:

And when abundance and generosity are lacking, our attendees use words like this:

In which of these two very different workplaces would *you* prefer to spend roughly one-third of your life? (Yes, we know that's a loaded question. But we're just making sure you're still with us here. Are you?)

When you come from a place of abundance and generosity, you look at the world as a glass-half-full kind of place—a joyous, infinite game. You believe there's plenty of success to go around, so why not share it with others—with your allies and even those you don't like so much. (There are always at least a few in every workplace!)

In this chapter, we'll dive deep into this practice and discover how it can help you achieve an Ally Mindset.

Abundance: Having Everything You Need and More

When you have an abundance mindset, you feel that there is plenty to share with others, whether it's time, money, people, information, expertise, or any number of other valuable things in a particular situation or environment. It's the opposite of a scarcity mindset. Those who work from a scarcity mindset in a business may believe, for example, that there are a limited number of clients out there in the world, so they may keep information about these clients away from their "competitors" inside the organization, which often leads to politics, silos, and turf wars. They're looking out for *me*, not *we*. We're going to take a wild guess that you've experienced this kind of toxic competition for yourself because we *all* have.

At best, it's a zero-sum, finite game that keeps you stuck. At worst, it becomes a race to be the first to eat the pie, which creates lots of indigestion and heartburn (and other less pleasant gastrointestinal side effects) all around.

But when you look at the world with an abundance mindset, you see a glass half-full of opportunities. These opportunities may come my way, or they may come your way, but we grow when we work together to execute on them. In doing so, we move from a scarcity-driven, fear-based mindset that minimizes opportunities to an abundance-driven, generosity-based mindset that maximizes opportunities. We have *fun* and generate success as we bake the pie together, instead of trying to be the first to eat it. We ensure there's a piece for everyone, which results in a bigger pie (and waistline!) for the entire organization.

It's a clear win-win if ever there was one.

Executive coach Marshall Goldsmith is a remarkable example of someone who has created a lot of tremendously valuable intellectual property over the course of his long career and who maintains an abundance mindset about it. He imparts his decades' worth of coaching wisdom for free through his 100 Coaches organization, and he also gives away all his intellectual property through his Knowledge Philanthropy project. No fees, no licensing, no asking for permission, no "pretty pleases" required. And if you want to take his words, rewrite them, and use them as your own, Goldsmith invites you to do just that if that's what floats your boat.

The good news for Goldsmith is that his abundance mindset will undoubtedly allow him to have an even greater impact on the world than if he had held on to his intellectual property tightly and fought anyone who tried to use it.

An abundance mindset changes your perspective on life, at work and play. Morag describes it like this:

> An abundance mindset encourages me to be bold, to think (and dream) big.
>
> When I operate with a mindset of abundance and generosity, and my personal definition of success, I reduce the self-imposed stress about not doing enough that can come

from comparing myself to others. There's enough success for all. This empowers us to have fun at work, to push ourselves and our clients outside our comfort zones and create amazing results—together.

If I'm not comparing myself to you (as much) or trying to keep up with the Joneses, then I can focus on being the best version of me. I am enough.

When I recognize that I am enough, I find I have a more solid foundation from which I can learn and grow, reducing the trash talk that can and does self-sabotage all of us.

An abundance mindset drives healthy competition; I'm continuously learning and growing with Eric and Ruby, rather than trying to beat them to the finish line. It allows us to have fun at work (part of our corporate values) and challenge each other.

An abundance mindset is truly empowering. The opportunities abound, especially when I don't feel like I have to win every single time (unless it's a game of Scrabble with my brother, in which case all bets are off).

I've lost count of the number of times that others— clients, colleagues, leaders—have commented on how much they appreciate our support and willingness to go the extra mile, and it's one of the (many) reasons they keep coming back to SkyeTeam. Abundance and generosity are recognized and appreciated.

One of our clients is an old-line company that has been put through the ringer with all the change going on in its markets. While some of the people we work with on one of the company's teams have been there fifteen or more years, others have been around only a couple of months. And over the last few years, most of the folks on the team have had several different bosses. There have been multiple reorganizations, and

Every time you
give, every time you
pay it forward,
you create a ripple in
the world around you.

these reorganizations have naturally created and reinforced a scarcity mindset within the team. People want to hang on to what they have, and abundance is a very distant and faraway place—mostly long forgotten.

Within this team, people hoard information. They don't talk to one another. They intentionally prevent other teams from being successful to make their own team look good, even though it kills the other team's ability to achieve their goals and harms the organization. The team looks bad in front of the customer but looks good to themselves. Just listening to members of the team talk about how it all works kind of blows our minds because, in that mindset, they believe they're doing the right thing—the *only* thing. They defend their choices and actions, even though they know they're not getting the outcomes they want. But they're hung up on control, and it's true: the less abundance you feel, the more control you feel you need.

Which brings us to some very deep questions for this client: Why here? Why now? Why for *so many* years?

In this case, one major complicating factor for this team is ongoing turnover at the executive level. The team's top executive invariably quits after only about twelve months on the job, and this has been the case for years. So, every time a new leader walks in the door and takes charge, they'll say, "Here's what we're going to do..." And everybody goes, "Sure, we've heard that one before. We'll just bide our time and keep doing what we've always done. Within a year you'll be gone and there will be a brand-new person in charge." It's a self-fulfilling cycle with no end, and a failure for the team.

Fortunately, we were able to work with the latest leader of this team—who had not been in place very long—and it was clear to us that he was facing a very difficult situation. (It was like pushing a growing boulder up an increasingly steep hill!)

We knew that to be successful, he would need to commit to changing the team's scarcity mindset to one of abundance, and this would have to start with him—he would have to walk his talk. This meant not just using words to tell his team what his expectations were but also modeling these expectations and rewarding employees when they acted on them. As recognition expert Dr. Bob Nelson shared with us, "What gets recognized gets repeated."

The good news is that the team is finally, after all these years, beginning to transform in the way they should have long ago. Better late than never.

Changing from a scarcity mindset to an abundance mindset is a heavy lift in a burdened culture like this one, but it can—and it must—be done. Not sure how? Professor and vulnerability guru Brené Brown suggests that a good place to start is by engaging in our lives from "a place of worthiness." According to Brown, "It means cultivating the courage, compassion, and connection to wake up in the morning and think, 'No matter what gets done and how much is undone, I am enough.' It's going to bed at night thinking, 'Yes, I am imperfect and vulnerable and sometimes afraid, but that doesn't change the truth that I am also brave and worthy of love and belonging.'"

Ultimately, abundance is understanding that if something is to be, it begins with *me*. Remember, it's not about asking, "Do I have best friends at work?" It's about asking, "Am I a best friend at work?" Don't wait for others to shower their abundance on you—you might be waiting a very long time. Be the one to take the first step, and every step after that. Be the leader, the coworker, the friend, the neighbor, the significant other that *you* wish you had in your business and personal life. Set the bar high and invite others to follow your example.

Generosity: Fearlessly Giving

What holds so many of us back from being more generous? In our experience, it's because we naturally operate with a scarcity mindset instead of an abundance mindset. We're afraid of not having enough to look after ourselves, and so we hoard information, we hoard money, we hoard networks of connections with others, and we hoard anything else of value. It's a *me-first* instead of a *we-first* mindset. It's all about fear—fear of not having enough, fear of not being enough, fear of rejection, fear of not being good enough.

Many of us have come up during some rough economic times. Says Eric:

> If I had a dollar for every time I was scared shitless of losing my job, I could pay for this book! When I graduated college in 1992, the economy sucked so I went to grad school. I graduated from that in 1995, and things were not much better. I started my own business in 2005, right before the Great Recession kicked into gear, and then I went to work at Level 3 Communications, where we had a layoff the first Friday of every month for three years. After that, I did two startups—one went okay, one did not. Until I joined Skye-Team in 2012, the practice of abundance and generosity was not part of my operating system, and I acted accordingly. I was very much *me-first* focused. It didn't take long for the shift to happen; when you see it in action every day, it's easier to adopt the *we-first* focus!

Here's another example: when Charlene called Morag, it was to ask for guidance on how to price a workshop she was preparing for a senior leadership team. Charlene is an executive coach, used to working one-to-one; leading a group event was not something she did regularly. The conversation quickly moved from how much to charge to brainstorming the content and flow for the event. As she and Morag spoke, several red flags came up. They tweaked the activities Charlene had planned to ensure they would strengthen the relationships within the team and not inflame an already stressed-out team. By the end of the conversation, Charlene sounded positively excited about the upcoming event.

Charlene's text to Morag following the workshop read: "Huge thank you. Not only did you help me design the session, but you also gave me the gift of confidence. It went beautifully. At the end, the person who hired me gave me a hug. Another leader hired me on the spot."

This is abundance and generosity in action. A thirty-minute call that expanded into ninety minutes—that didn't just focus on *what* needed to be done but also *how* Charlene would lead the session—increased her confidence and ultimately helped her shine.

Every time you give, every time you pay it forward, you create a ripple in the world around you—in your people, in your clients and customers, in your suppliers and vendors, and in the communities in which you do business. Make enough ripples, and you can have a real impact. If you're not sure how to make those ripples, or your skills are a bit rusty, executive coach Howard H. Prager's book, *Make Someone's Day*, is a great resource—chock-full of examples and short exercises for... making someone's day. Writes Prager, "The most powerful words someone can say to you are 'You made my day!' You haven't just done an act of kindness when you hear that. You have done something, at the right time and in the right way, that's the most powerful tool for inspiring your colleagues, staff, friends and even strangers. As a result, you may turn someone's day or life around, inspire and motivate them, or simply get them unstuck."

When you take care
of yourself, you're
better able to take
care of others.

Generosity doesn't only come in the form of money; it comes from sharing your knowledge and experiences, coaching and mentoring others. It also comes from being generous with your time. Our friend Barbara O'Dwyer is a role model for generosity, regularly opening her home to host others—whether it's family, SkyeTeam events, or Morag's fiftieth birthday party. Her generosity is only matched by the boundless energy of Mack.

Mack is Barb's labradoodle, and together they trained and now volunteer as a therapy dog team at a local hospital. Before and during the pandemic, Barb and Mack were tireless in their support of healthcare workers, providing much-needed and often-requested respite from the day-to-day stresses that are part and parcel of treating COVID-19 patients. They are on call to visit with end-of-life patients and their families and are often in the room during these solemn moments, providing emotional support to all.

They are such a successful team that Barb now coordinates the entire therapy dog group. And they recently extended their generosity by completing crisis training, which means they will be called out in response to major disasters. All this generous giving of their time is unpaid, and the impact is immense.

At the end of your life, or at the end of your time at a company, what do you want to be remembered for? Do you want to be remembered as a generous, go-to person who graciously helps others out of a pickle? Do you want to be remembered as the leader who builds others up rather than tears them down? Do you want to be remembered as someone who inspires others to dream big dreams and continues to raise the bar on delivering value to customers?

We do.

When graduates of our programs call and say, "Hey, I've moved on to a different organization, but I have a question..."

Hell yeah, we have an answer for them. We're *family*; we have a connection. It's an infinite game for us—we are committed to playing the game as long as we can. And we do.

We have made a habit of hanging out after our workshops to talk with participants in a casual setting. It's gotten to the point where we block out the time after the virtual workshops on our schedules because we know from our experience that three or four people will stop by to ask questions—either about the topic or about how it relates to what they're working on. This is the pandemic world equivalent of the hallway conversations or "clearing the room" moments we participate in live on-site. We'll spend time talking with people to help them solve their real-world leadership challenges because we like these folks. We feel *connected*. (More on this topic in the next chapter.)

Generosity is related to abundance but distinctly different. It's giving to others freely without expectation of getting anything back in return or keeping count. It's akin to lighting someone else's candle. The act of lighting their candle doesn't diminish your own light; in fact, it makes us all shine a little bit brighter. If abundance is about *being*, then generosity is about *doing*.

We have to admit that we have a little bit of a crush on Wharton professor and bestselling author Adam Grant. His insights on the world of work are profound. What's not to like? Anyway, Grant provides perspective on both abundance and generosity: "In healthy relationships, both people give and receive with no strings attached. They grant each other the freedom to ask without shame, accept without obligation, and decline without guilt."

Grant also shared his own example of abundance and generosity: "In grad school, on my first major paper, I wanted to include 2 undergraduates as coauthors. An advisor told me it was a mistake. I agreed, and coauthored the paper with 5 undergraduates instead. Sharing credit with others takes nothing away from you."

However, Grant also has a cautionary note about generosity that is good to keep in mind. In a Facebook post, he wrote, "Generosity isn't saying yes to every request. It's helping when you can make a unique contribution. Generosity isn't sacrificing yourself for others. It's helping when it won't exhaust you—and when it energizes you."

This comes back to what being an ally means. First, you define it for yourself using a framework, using your own language—what do you stand for, and given what is being asked of you personally and professionally today, what can you say yes to and what do you need to say no to?

True generosity is all about getting the balance right—for you and for others. You don't *always* need to say yes to be generous with your time, energy, funds, and other resources. In fact, you need to reserve some generosity for yourself too. When you take care of yourself, you're better able to take care of others.

We All Have the Same 168 Hours a Week

In his book *Your 168*, Harry Kraemer explores the answer to the question, How do you play an infinite game in a finite-resourced world? If we all work within the same time limitations, why do we have such wildly varying outcomes? According to Kraemer, "No matter who you are, what you do for a living, where you live, or how productive you are, you only get 168 hours a week. The only difference is how you spend that time."

Kraemer suggests dividing up your time into life buckets, including such things as career, family, faith/spirituality, health/sleep, fun/recreation/reading, and making a difference. And instead of just focusing on career, Kraemer believes that—to live a values-based life—you need to plan for and be accountable for how you spend *all* of your 168 hours.

This is abundance and generosity at work—playing the infinite game in a finite world. It's knowing that there *is* a finite amount of time, there is a finite budget, there is a finite number of CEOs in your company (i.e., *one*). When everyone is going for that same promotion, there are going to be, in the old terminology, winners and losers. But how do you celebrate the winners, even if they're not you? Generosity is about the willingness to give—to celebrate *everyone's* successes. As author and researcher Ruth Gotian asks, "Can competitors be friends or go so far as being collaborators? Can they support each other's success with pride and admiration? Of course, they can, and it makes each person's work more potent and better, richer and brimming with innovative ideas."

At SkyeTeam, when we partner with a client, there is invariably scope creep. It's part of what we love—bringing our minds together and creating something even better than we first envisioned. And it's our abundance mindset that enables this better outcome to emerge. Of course, if the scope continues to grow, at some point we have to say, "No, that's a new statement of work." That's not selfish. That allows us to be selfless with our 168 hours, to make sure that we are meeting our needs while also helping clients to achieve theirs. Boundaries are healthy, they're a good thing, and they're critical in showing up as an ally.

In these situations, abundance and generosity is proactive— particularly when you're a leader. Great leaders are always pushing their people to grow and to try new things. They believe in others even before those people believe in themselves. It's about working with your employees, getting to know them beyond their job titles, and making sure they feel well taken care of.

Ruby worked as a pastoral assistant to one such leader, Father Brian, who fully lived this practice of abundance and generosity. One of the things he would always say in his homilies was "God will never be outdone in generosity." And Father Brian set the bar high in his own life; he really took care of his parishioners and staff. Says Ruby:

> I remember we had one staff member whose kids were in school, and Father Brian knew that she didn't have enough money for groceries. He would have us buy gift cards and then give them to her anonymously. Another time someone needed money to help pay their college tuition, and Father Brian found donors who were able to make that possible! He also founded our parish food bank that to this day still serves hundreds of families at any given time. As a leader, he was always proactively looking for ways to care for and be in service to others. In turn, this cultivated a heart of service leadership in each of our staff members, volunteers, and the larger community.

When you give generously to someone, it expands generosity in your team, in your community, and in the world in a circular way. When you put abundance and generosity out there, it generates a response in others to do the same—to give to others, to pay it forward. In short, the more generous people are, the more generous people are. As Mark Twain once said, "If you want love and abundance in your life, give it away."

Pivoting from *Me* First to *We* First

Two leaders (one in charge of product and the other in charge of operations) in an organization were not allies; for whatever reason, they were archrivals who both lacked an abundance and generosity mindset. This antagonism was expressed as hoarding information "to get one over on the other" and seeking to win favor with their bosses (and maybe a fat bonus or stock option grant) by championing their own projects.

The product leader presented his idea for a cool new product to the executive team, and he was granted the funds necessary to build and test it. He had deliberately left the operations leader out of the loop to improve, he thought, the chances that the product would be approved. Everyone was impressed with the product leader's presentation and thought it had the potential to become a great future revenue generator for the company.

Well, everyone except for one person.

The operations leader was furious with this outcome, and when the product was handed over from production to the live environment, suddenly there were bugs and defects and it "didn't appear to work." *That* made the operations leader feel much better! He showed the product leader who the boss was!

Sadly, this overt lack of abundance and generosity didn't just sabotage the product, it also sabotaged the reputations and careers of these two leaders and the future growth prospects for the company. As much as they thought they were wearing their best poker faces (isn't there a Lady Gaga song about that?) and keeping their turf battles a secret, the simple truth was that *everyone* knew.

For mid-level managers, abundance and generosity are important. Think of it this way: up to this point in a career,

The longer a person waits
to pivot from *me* to *we*,
the larger the gap between
where they are as a leader and
where they need to be.

most everything a person has achieved will have been through their own efforts. They've been in the mode of *me* first in terms of their education and early career as an individual contributor. They were told what to do, went away and did it, then came back and got promoted. Now, however, after making it to this lofty point in a career, it's time to realize that everything has changed.

From this day forward, everything a person does has to be about the *we* mindset and not a *me* mindset, because their success is dependent on their ability to achieve good outcomes with and through others.

"But how?" you ask.

A person does this by delegating to their team, coaching and mentoring them, and collaborating horizontally with their peers. And if they don't make this vital pivot in their career as a manager, then they're not going to have the abundance and generosity they need to thrive and grow and succeed in the long run. The longer a person waits to pivot from *me* to *we*, the larger the gap between where they are as a leader and where they need to be. This gap will continue to grow and be more difficult to overcome as they become a manager of a manager and then progress to more senior positions.

For juniors in an organization, there are likely people— perhaps their bosses or coworkers—who are abundant in generosity to support and guide them. At least we hope there are. These juniors may not even notice it after a while; the mentoring their boss is providing and the assistance the members of their team are offering are the wallpaper of an organization's culture. If all of a sudden this culture changed to one of scarcity and *me* first instead of *we* first, they would definitely notice and we're certain they wouldn't like it one little bit.

Remember, the practice of abundance and generosity is not about keeping count—it's all a thread.

What can you do to remove a barrier, to provide an opportunity, to give feedback, to offer guidance, to lift someone's spirits? This goes far beyond random acts of kindness because it's not random when it becomes part of your everyday routine. When you look for opportunities to help others shine, then you also get to bask in that glory and *everyone* shines. It's the candle thing again—lighting someone else's candle takes nothing away from your candle. It makes us all shine brighter. So, why not do it?

One of our favorite examples of a leader who fully embraces the abundance and generosity mindset is Michael Gartner, the former majority owner and chairman of the Iowa Cubs minor league baseball team. Like every other sports team (and for all of us!), 2020 was a particularly difficult year for the Cubs. On June 30, the league canceled its 2020 season. This put the more than one hundred minor league teams—which were already suffering because of quarantines and uncertainty resulting from the COVID-19 pandemic—in dire financial straits.

Most team owners felt they had no choice but to lay off or furlough their employees as COVID-19 raged throughout the year. And the cancellation of the 2020 season was just the icing on a very putrid, half-baked cake that even the Cake Boss couldn't rescue.

But there was a notable exception to this terrible train of events: the Iowa Cubs. Said Michael Gartner, "We kept everybody on full pay and benefits the whole time. We lost $4 million, but they needed the money more than I did." Talk about having an abundance mindset! Rather than putting his employees out on the street to fend for themselves, Gartner thought of them as *family*—valued individuals who needed the team's help and support.

In addition to earning the gratitude and no doubt even greater loyalty of his people, Gartner's decision paid other dividends. While other minor league teams had to scramble to rehire employees in anticipation of the 2021 season—often finding that those employees had moved on and were no longer available, making recruiting particularly difficult—the Cubs already had their staff in place and ready to go. According to Gartner, "To get ready for [opening day], I didn't really have to do anything. I've got all these great people who work here."

As if that wasn't enough, as a final gesture of generosity following the sale of the Cubs in 2021, Gartner and his associates shared the profits by handing out checks to every full-time employee based on tenure, totaling $600,000.

You don't have to give away buckets of money to have an abundant and generous mindset. The question, however, is this: What can you do at your level? How can you put abundance and generosity to work for you, for your people, for your customers, for your organization, and for the communities in which you do business? What can you do right now to begin to enjoy the benefits of the Ally Mindset—of which abundance and generosity are an integral part?

It comes back to understanding what you do and don't stand for, and being aware of the needs of the people around you. And playing the infinite game for as long as you possibly can.

LOOK UP, SHOW UP, STEP UP

As the old saying goes, what gets planned gets done. If you've taken the Ally Mindset Profile (you *have* taken it by now, right?) and you learned that you're lacking when it comes to abundance and generosity, then we strongly suggest that you plan to be more abundant and generous. But that's just a start. Here are some proven approaches that could form the heart of your plan:

- **Beware the scarcity mindset.** When you feel yourself becoming defensive, or fighting for your point of view, pause. Instead of reacting and defending your turf, reconnect with your values, then channel your curiosity and focus on how you can adjust going forward in support of your goals. When faced with someone who has a scarcity mindset, remain curious as to their point of view to better identify and communicate mutual needs and expectations to move the relationship forward.

- **Make abundance and generosity a daily habit.** Make it a point to catch someone doing something right—to acknowledge the good things they've done. Whether it's a handwritten note or a comment on a social media post, in person, or by phone, give heartfelt thanks to the people who help you accomplish your own goals.

- **Take a long slow look in the mirror.** An Ally Mindset isn't only about looking out for and supporting others. It is also about taking the time to look inward and ensure you are attending to your own needs, dreams, wants. This isn't selfishness; this is selflessness. Invest the time in reflecting on what you are grateful for, what you hope to achieve (tomorrow, next week, next year), and plan the actions that will help you continue to attract and radiate abundance and generosity.

Take some time to reflect on the following questions:

- Who are the role models in your life and what do they do or not do to demonstrate this practice? What does demonstrating abundance and generosity look like for you?

- Are you protecting your stores or are you opening the doors? Abundance and generosity are the first pivot from *me* first to *we* first. Challenge your initial reactions to circumstances.

- How do you define success? When are you enough? When will you have achieved enough? Without this insight, how do you know when to say "no thank you" or to give a heartfelt "heck yes"?

- What are you ready and willing to do more of, less of, or say no to?

CONNECTION AND COMPASSION

Empathy *Rules*!

66

When we focus on others, our world
expands. Our own problems drift
to the periphery of the mind and so
seem smaller, and we increase our capacity
for connection—or compassionate action.

DANIEL GOLEMAN

I T'S NO SECRET that humans are hardwired for *connection* with one another; it's built into our DNA and reinforced with every positive relationship we enjoy during our lives. Building an Ally Mindset requires *really* connecting with people in the workplace, including coworkers, customers, vendors, even our boss. (Perhaps *especially* with our boss—the one who signs our paychecks!)

But the Ally Mindset requires more than connection. It also requires *compassion*—having empathy for the highs and lows of those you connect with and being able to put yourself in their shoes. You cheer their successes and mourn their losses—even with your competitors, who can also be your friends and collaborators. You build them up when they most need your support. You give them some slack when they're at the end of their rope. You habitually practice *radical humanity*, assuming positive intent on the part of others and putting people before profits. And oh, by the way, it takes happy, engaged people to make profits.

Early in Ruby's career—at data storage company Seagate Technology, what she calls her first "big girl job"—her father was diagnosed with stage 4 cancer. Sadly, he passed away just six months later. The silver lining of this story is that

Ruby had the remarkably good fortune to be part of a highly connected team at work that was filled to overflowing with compassion. It was spilling out all over the place! Here's how she describes the difficult months after her father's diagnosis:

> My personal life was a hot mess: I was navigating my early twenties working two jobs while balancing my time to see my dad as much as I could. There were the roller-coaster ups and downs of two failed chemo treatments, intermittent hospital stays, good days, bad days, and completely-losing-my-shit days. But I was able to be there with my dad for the moments that counted.
>
> Throughout all of that, my manager and my colleagues supported me every single step of the way. I was not coddled or "taken care of." Instead, I was shown true empathy, connection, and compassion. I had the flexibility in my work to go visit my father every day at lunch and leave when I needed to get to my second job—yet I was still held accountable for the work that needed to be done.
>
> And after my father passed, every single one of my team members were at his funeral. When I gave the eulogy, I looked out over the crowd and saw my family, my father's coworkers, and my colleagues—my true best friends at work.
>
> My team grieved with me. My team celebrated the highs with me. My team laughed with me and cried with me. They cared about me as a human. This meant everything, and that time in my career has forever changed me as a leader. When we meet others with true connection and compassion, the ripple effects are infinite.

Connection and compassion are built in everyday interactions, through recognition and acknowledgment, when we feel that we are seen, that our voices are heard, and that our opinions matter. We feel connected when we are treated as more than a job title or a cog in the wheel of an organization, when we have psychological safety. We feel connection when we go through the ups and downs of life and business together, and when we show compassion for members of our team, our customers, and for the communities in which we do business.

In her book *Braving the Wilderness*, Brené Brown explained, "The more we are willing to seek out moments of collective joy and show up for experiences of collective pain—for real, in person, not online—the more difficult it becomes to deny our human connection, even with people we disagree with. Not only do moments of human connection remind us of what is possible between people, but they also remind us of what is true about the human spirit. We are wired for connection."

When there is connection and compassion in our workplaces, our workshop attendees use these words to describe it:

Connection and compassion strengthen your professional ties and lend the courage to remove your professional mask and share what is really going on for you.

And when connection and compassion are missing? It's not a pretty sight—not at all. These words don't just look creepy and cold, they *feel* creepy and cold:

COLD GUARDED EMPTY ISOLATED DISCONNECTED LIFELESS DEPRESSING IMPERSONAL LONELY UNHEARD

Despite what you may have been led to believe by some overzealous experiential consultant (doing their darndest to boost their bottom line), connection and compassion don't come from group hugs and trust falls and ropes courses. (Have you tried them? How did *that* work out?) Other than the risk of a sprained ankle or bruised ego to carry forward, experiences such as these rarely create lasting change in the strength of team relationships. According to a study of 223 executives reported in the MIT *Sloan Management Review*, "76 percent reported that they had difficulty making connections with their work teammates, and 58 percent agreed with the statement 'My social relationships are superficial at work.'" Clearly it takes something much deeper than a single team-building session to move the needle when it comes to connection and compassion.

Garry Ridge, chairman and CEO at WD-40 Company, makes no secret of the importance of relationships to his success and the success of the organization. In a conversation with Morag, Garry shared how the organization shifted its culture to a people-first orientation that would "set people free" and create a "high will of the people." As he explained, we all have a desire to belong, and we have all left a company, event, or relationship because we didn't feel that sense of belonging. WD-40 Company created its unique, people-first culture to address this basic human need. The following, from the company's 2021 annual report, sums this up:

> Our tribe = our success. We are a tribe, and as a tribe we're here for each other as much as we're here for the company. Our definition of tribe is a community of people with a shared purpose who help feed and defend each other. We're here to support, protect, nurture, and help each other grow while we work together to create positive lasting memories for all our stakeholders around the globe.

When it comes to role-modeling an Ally Mindset, WD-40 Company focuses on relationships, connection, and compassion; those practices are at the heart of everything they do, and we love it.

In this chapter, we'll show you how to use connection and compassion to create and nurture stronger relationships with others, as you continue to build your Ally Mindset.

Connection: You Build Relationships

At its very essence, *connection* is all about the relationships you build with others. Some work connections may be weak—just a passing acquaintance you meet at the coffee table at the back of the room while waiting for a conference to start—while others may be remarkably strong, such as the bond many form with bosses or certain coworkers and customers. According to Brené Brown (we *love* her, can you tell?), connection is "the energy that exists between people when they feel seen, heard, and valued; when they can give and receive without judgment; and when they derive sustenance and strength from the relationship."

The Four Yeses are four questions we ask ourselves in every relationship. (We'll talk more about these questions in chapter 9). They are the glue that holds together the five parts of the Ally Mindset Framework (and the WD-40 that keeps relationships moving effortlessly):

1 Can I count on you?
2 Can I depend on you?
3 Do I care about you?
4 Do I trust you?

To establish, grow, and sustain connections with others over a long period of time, we must be able to answer yes to each of these four questions. In this framework, people being able to count on you is about what you do regularly, systematically, to establish trust with others; people learn to depend on you when you respond proactively to their needs. When I can count on you (and you on me), we build connection. When I can depend on you (and you on me), we build connection. When I care about you (and I can show you that I care about you), we build connection. When I trust you (and I can make you feel safe to trust me), we build connection.

And when *you* can count on me, when you can depend on me, when you care about me, when you trust me, well, then there is no stopping the power of *us*. We have connection and we are likely to have compassion—a relationship based on mutual respect. When *me* first becomes *we* first, then you have a true multiplier effect.

If we haven't connected at the human level, then we're going to have a really tough time dealing with the difficult conversations that will inevitably come later on. And now that many organizations are moving to hybrid workplaces with employees working at least part-time at home, making and maintaining connections with others require intentionality, care, and attention. The change is already happening: the future *will* be more hybrid.

We've already shared that Morag was born and raised in England, and we realize that it can be a bit of a challenge to hear the nuances when you are reading her words in a book— tomayto, tomahto, potaytoe, potahtoe. However, trust us, the accent is real and you've already experienced some of her "colourful" metaphors in the stories we've shared. And trust us when we tell you that what you've heard about British reserve and stiff upper lip is all true. Morag often shares how she would differentiate between her work life and home life. Never the twain should meet, and as for communicating her true thoughts and feelings, it was always a filtered Morag that she shared with others. Explains Morag:

> In business situations, I always presented a crisp, got-my-shit-together mask. Professional at all times. It was interesting when I moved from the UK to the US; even learning to hug versus shake hands when greeting others was a big adjustment for me. I continued to keep things bottled up, battened down, and squared away. I'd perfected a defensive wall between me and the outside world. One that protected me from sharing my thoughts and feelings. One that focused on you because in doing so I didn't need to look inward, at me.
>
> This finally broke down when I received some very specific feedback from a C-level executive I was coaching. I

knew everything about him—his trials, his tribulations, his stresses, and much more. (This is a common situation because our clients confide in the three of us very quickly about what's happening at work and home.) The problem was, I didn't necessarily reciprocate. The working relationship I established with the executive felt to him unbalanced, and he told me that.

At that moment, I realized I needed to share the highs and lows of my own life experiences in support of others, not the safe, edited highlights I had been sharing until then. It feels strange and uncomfortable (to me) as I flex this new muscle, as I embrace all of life's emotions instead of leaving some of them safely boxed up on a shelf at home. In doing so, the sky hasn't fallen, and in fact several people have commented that I seemed even brighter and more vibrant and more in the moment than usual.

It makes me chuckle to realize that everything I have been championing for others I need to do too! I take my own medicine when I bring my whole true self to work, and I no longer feel like I have to pretend or filter. I can give you 85 percent of Morag—because there's still 15 percent you shouldn't see—versus you only getting 50 percent of Morag, and it's better for everyone. There's a connection. We bring our human to work.

According to a recent McKinsey survey, nine out of ten organizations are moving to a hybrid model of work. The survey also confirmed that worker productivity and customer satisfaction both increased during the COVID-19 pandemic. Why? According to McKinsey, it's because of the power of connection: "According to our survey, [high-productivity companies are] the ones supporting small connections between colleagues—opportunities to discuss projects, share ideas, network, mentor, and coach, for example. Two-thirds of productivity leaders report that these kinds of 'microtransactions' have increased, compared with just 9 percent of productivity laggards. As executives look to sustain pandemic-style productivity gains with a hybrid model, they will need to design and develop the right spaces for these small interactions to take place."

Connection is undeniably important, but like many other things in work and life, it's not the *quantity* of connections you make that will ultimately have the greatest impact; it's the *quality* of them. Research reveals that one in four Americans report having no one they can confide in, call on in an emergency, or describe as a best friend. So, starting with having one trusted ally is enough. According to Yale professor Marissa King, "Decades of research has shown that the myopic focus on network size is misguided. The *quality* (not *quantity*) of your social connections is a strong predictor of your cognitive functioning, work resilience, and work engagement."

Not only that, but the quality and nature of your connections at work can impact how much you are paid, the likelihood of your hearing about a new idea, whether a venture capitalist will fund your new startup, the level of your success on the job, and the extent of your own emotional and physical well-being.

Consider the advice of Michelle Tillis Lederman, author of *The Connector's Advantage*: "Show your people you care about them as people and that you care about the things they care about. The result is engagement, loyalty, productivity, retention and a better bottom line."

The connections you create and nurture make a significant difference in your life and in the lives of others around you. Social connection is the predictor of long-term happiness in life, which is why we should seek it out. One thing to keep

The connections you
create and nurture make
a significant difference
in your life and in the lives
of others around you.

in mind: if you have been blindsided or taken by surprise by the words, actions, or deeds of someone, then that is a clear indication that you don't have a strong connection with the person. It's up to you to reach out and get to know them at a human level.

Compassion: You Give It to Yourself and Others

When we talk about connection, we also need to talk about compassion. Compassion is the authentic desire to help others and to have a positive impact. Remember abundance and generosity in the previous chapter? When we have a mindset of abundance and generosity, we feel more compassion toward others. These components build on one another, so buckle up!

We need to show compassion toward others—give them the benefit of the doubt, assume positive intent, look at the world through a glass-half-full prism. And we need to show compassion toward ourselves—self-compassion is *huge*! We often beat ourselves up and trash talk ourselves in a way we would never do to others.

Think about a time when you really whiffed the ball, you snafued, missed the mark—you know, you just blew it. What did you say to yourself? What was the language that you used when talking to yourself about this huge miss? Chances are it consisted of words not suitable for church and were probably things that you would not say to another human being's face. Whoever said "we are our own worst critics" was putting it mildly at best. As Jack Kornfield once wrote, "If your compassion does not include yourself, it is incomplete."

In an *Entrepreneur* article, Aytekin Tank—founder and CEO of Jotform—describes how a lack of self-compassion affected him, threatening to derail all he had accomplished:

I remember sitting in the middle of a tech conference years ago when I first founded my company, Jotform. I watched as, one by one, established entrepreneurs took turns in sharing their stories of success. Every time one would get up to speak, I heard this small, nagging voice in my head tell me: *You're not good enough.*

I had fallen into the trap of comparison and self-pity, which then led to a snowball effect of self-criticism. *Why can't I reach my goals faster? Why am I the only one struggling to scale up my startup?*

Not only was I beating myself up over my perceived shortcomings, I wasn't seeing the whole picture.

At SkyeTeam, we get to work with some really cool teams and leaders, across industries and from around the world. All are working to achieve amazing results; however, their leadership styles don't always best serve to achieve these results. One such leader who comes to mind is Steve.

Steve was a leader who valued candor and debate, qualities that we explore in chapter 6. He was a quick thinker and not shy to point out the flaws in the plans or projects of others. Unfortunately, he was low on connection and compassion—the soft and fluffy stuff he thought best left to HR. Group hugs and trust falls weren't his thing (they aren't ours either), but he was missing the point. He was a lone ranger—my way or the highway. Steve achieved results but with the inevitable "cleanup on aisle thirteen" outcome to his professional relationships.

Oblivious to the churn left in his wake, he continued with his high candor-low connection, high action-low compassion ways. After all, everything (except for the feedback he wasn't getting) was telling him he was successful *because* of this fast-paced style. Results were coming in, and while he was a little rough around the edges, that was just "Steve being Steve."

But it couldn't last.

The proverbial shit hit the fan. A big project missed deadlines, and other department heads went to the CEO, frustrated with Steve's lack of collaboration and listening skills. Suddenly Steve's approach wasn't looking so good, and something had to be done to correct it. Either that, or he would be eventually out of the organization and out of a job. Eric was brought in to help coach Steve, because the CEO realized he couldn't allow Steve to fail.

To give Steve his due, through his coaching conversations with Eric, he became vigilant—asking questions instead of barking orders, and remaining curious far longer than he had in the past to observe and adjust to the new rules of engagement. He was focused on unlearning and relearning new habits. Checking on *how* others were doing (not just *what* they were doing). Slowing down to ask a few clarifying questions to understand others' points of view, celebrating others' successes to share the limelight, and closing the feedback loop to ensure everyone was aligned and working together.

Six months after Eric started working with Steve, we conducted a stakeholder review, and the results couldn't have been more different. He was judged as firm but fair, approachable yet determined.

Steve was grateful: he recognized he was close to permanently damaging his relationships within the company. If this trajectory had continued, his career would have at best stalled and at worst flamed out. Instead he found himself looking forward to going to work, and others looked forward to working with him. Quite a turn of events.

We sincerely believe that people don't show up at work to be jerks or to do bad jobs or to annoy you. We all have bad days; it happens. Compassion recognizes that we have off days and that there are things outside of work that impact how we show up. We don't need to blindly excuse any behavior, but we need to acknowledge circumstances and hold people accountable to clear expectations.

Compassion is also what you show when others build connection by sharing their emotions—their fear and anxiety, as well as their joy and excitement—and you respond in kind, without judgment. Never take your feelings, or those of others, for granted. It takes courage to share them.

Connection and compassion strengthen your professional ties and lend you the courage to remove your professional mask and share what is really going on for you. This is true whether it's facing what's going on inside your head or interpersonally with friends, family, or colleagues. And while there are all sorts of good reasons for practicing compassion in your work and personal life, here are a few specific to organizations. Compassionate (and empathetic) workplaces tend to enjoy stronger collaboration, less stress, and greater morale, and their employees bounce back more quickly from difficult moments; they're more resilient. This all leads to a more engaged workforce and a stronger bottom line.

The questions about care and trust that we ask as part of the Four Yeses are all about compassion. People who define trust this way care about emotional, psychological, and physical safety. For them, trust is built when they know you will honor their emotions, support them, accept them no matter what they tell you, and not betray their confidence. Trust is eroded by failing to do these things. We'll talk more about trust in the next section.

We've worked with leaders who care deeply about their people, support them through thick and thin, yet cannot be counted on to do the tough work of accountability. (That

Making lasting
connections with others
requires trust.

is, they don't get a yes when a team member asks, "Can I count on you?" or "Can I depend on you?") Connection and compassion create the psychological safety and inclusion necessary to get the very best from your people—and to give your very best to others.

Trust: Not a Four-Letter Word

Making lasting connections with others requires *trust*. (We'll explore trust in more detail later; this is a quick preview.) People who are accomplished at making connections trust the people they work with, and they earn their trust in return. However, you must remember the Jedi mind trick of trust: to trust others, learn to trust yourself, you must. (Thanks, Master Yoda!) When you know how to put trust in yourself, you'll know how to put trust in others.

To give trust, you need to know what you stand for and what you don't stand for. And you must define and articulate the limits to which your abundance and generosity extend and what others can expect within those.

Trust opens us up to the risk of being hurt, but most of us are willing to take this risk. Why?

Because we want to connect with others. Because we *need* to connect with others—to do more, achieve more, be more. To be more *human*. But we need a firm foundation of trust to make those connections. Trust with a capital *T*.

The good news is that trust is a natural part of our long biological heritage—perhaps extending back through our primate ancestors and even beyond. If you have an animal companion—a dog, cat, horse, chicken, or even a rat—you know that you can build connection and bridges of trust with them too. Okay, we're not so sure about a chicken or a rat, but when your cat or dog flips over and lets you pet that sweet little belly, there's a huge amount of trust at play.

It's probably no big surprise to you that there has been a lot of research into the science of trust. What you may not know, however, is that much of this research has focused on the role of a very specific hormone: oxytocin. You may have seen this hormone referred to by a variety of different terms in the press: the bonding hormone, the cuddle hormone, and even the love hormone. We're going to let someone else write about those possibilities and keep our focus on trust.

One of the preeminent researchers on trust and oxytocin is Paul Zak. In a very scientific article for *Nature*, written in a very scientific way, Zak and a small army of coauthors explain that "trust pervades human societies. Trust is indispensable in friendship, love, families, and organizations." And we would argue that the reason trust is indispensable is because it enables us to establish, nurture, and grow connections with others.

So, what about oxytocin and the biological basis of trust? In the abstract for the *Nature* article, Zak and his colleagues explain that "intranasal administration of oxytocin, a neuropeptide that plays a key role in social attachment and affiliation in non-human mammals, causes a substantial increase in trust among humans, thereby greatly increasing the benefits from social interactions." So, when oxytocin is squirted up your nose and it finds its way into your bloodstream, your feelings of trust will increase, along with the feelings of connection you have with others.

In a TED Talk, Paul Zak described the experiment that led him and his colleagues to this discovery. Zak's hypothesis was that oxytocin would change the way that a group of test subjects—college students in this case—interacted with perfect strangers. At the beginning of the experiment, they gave each of the students ten dollars for participating. And then it started to get interesting. Said Zak in his TED Talk:

> Then we match them in pairs by computer. And in that pair, Person A gets a message saying, "Do you want to give up some of your ten dollars you earned for being here and ship it to someone else in the lab?" The trick is you can't see them, you can't talk to them. You only do it one time. Now whatever you give up gets tripled in the other person's account. You're going to make them a lot wealthier. And they get a message by computer saying Person A sent you this amount of money. Do you want to keep it all, or do you want to send some amount back?

So, what do you think happened? You might have guessed that the test subjects—both those who first sent money, and those who received money and were given the option of sending some back—would have tried to keep all the money for themselves. That's not how it played out. As it turned out, 90 percent of participants in the first group willingly sent some of their money to the other participant. This was a measure of the trust they felt for the other person.

What most surprised Zak and the other researchers, however, was that 95 percent of the people who received money in the first transaction sent some of it back. This was a measure of their trustworthiness. And guess what? The researchers found that the more oxytocin coursing through the bloodstreams of participants, the more trust there was. After some jabbing of needles and sampling of blood, Zak said, "By measuring oxytocin, we found that the more money the second person received, the more their brain produced oxytocin, and the more oxytocin on board, the more money they returned. So we have a biology of trustworthiness."

Long story short, the more oxytocin, the more trust. The more trust, the more connection we feel with others. The more connection we feel with others, the happier we are. And the happier we are, the more engaged we are in our work, the more loyal we are to our employer, and the greater value we create for our customers. It's a win-win all around.

You aren't going to go around injecting yourself with oxytocin (at least, *we* aren't!), so given that, how can you build bridges of trust with others? In her book *The Leadership Gap*, executive coach Lolly Daskal suggests that we can build bridges of trust by paying attention to four specific things: communication, commitment, competence, and character:

Communication. What's important is *how* people communicate—do they listen intently, or do they talk over others? Do they respond or do they react? How they communicate will determine whether or not we respect them.

Commitment. What's important is whether people keep their commitments. Their level of commitment will determine how we respond to them.

Competence. What's important is that people know what they are good at, and how their skills can contribute to making a difference. It is in competence that change will happen.

Character. What's important is your character. Who you are and how you act is where trust will be given, earned, and cultivated.

During the summer of 2019, we facilitated a team retreat for a group that was considered to be high performing. However, their stakeholder feedback indicated that while they were held in high regard for their individual results, the collective team was not seen as approachable. They were lacking *something*, the je ne sais quoi that would make them exceptional. Have you ever had feedback that vague and mushy? We have too. And with this kind of feedback, the team leader and members were at a loss.

We set about helping to fill the gap—conducting stakeholder interviews for specific examples of what the team had done to amaze and what they had not done so well. The team completed the Ally Mindset Profile, both as individuals and as a team.

As they reflected on the results, they had an epiphany: they lacked connection and compassion with their stakeholders and also a little within their team. They trusted one another to get their jobs done, but they didn't laugh very often—a huge indicator that there was a problem. There was no fun, no warmth, no human connection.

What did they do? They started checking in on how people were feeling within the team. They started checking in with stakeholders—not just on current projects but following up to see if their general needs were being met. They called when they didn't need something! They introduced a new way to start each team meeting, whether in person or online.

They now ask "What is one thing that is true for you today?" or "How are you doing—*really*?" Team members then either share out loud or reply in the chat. As the team reviews each response, they share their individual reactions:

- Snapping fingers: celebrating or acknowledging what was shared

- Palm facing out: I feel the same way; this really resonates with me

- Hand over heart: sending love and support

We were there to witness an early meeting where one of the team members shared that he was feeling "anxious and overwhelmed." Powerful words. The team rallied: there was no judgment or explanation required in the moment, just their reactions.

When we later spoke with the anxious team member, he confided that the reactions from his team had helped lower his stress level almost immediately. Just to know he was seen and heard and that he wasn't the only one having these feelings calmed his anxiety.

Think about this example for a minute. It can feel trite to do these human-connection exercises, to wonder if you should do them every day. (We vote yes; we do a version of this exercise at every SkyeTeam staff meeting.) Had the team not asked, they might never have known their colleague was close to a breaking point. He would have continued to feel isolated, alone, and disconnected from the team. Instead, in less than two minutes, the pressure was reduced, colleagues connected, and after the meeting conversations to provide support took place.

We all have a stress point where we need each other. Better to have your relationships in place and at the ready for when you need to call on others for their help and support. Start building bridges of trust while connecting and showing compassion to others. Put less emphasis on the bottom line and more emphasis on being human. It's our firm belief that when you focus on people first, the profits will follow.

As Dr. Michelle K. Johnston, professor of management and author of the book *The Seismic Shift in Leadership*, told us on the *People First!* podcast with Morag:

The old leadership characteristics of power, control, and fear are becoming more and more obsolete. Authenticity,

When you focus
on people first,
the profits will follow.

compassion, and alignment are the new paths to leadership success. Is power necessary to demonstrate confidence? Yes, absolutely. Is power necessary to project a strong presence when making presentations? Yes, absolutely. But power needs to be redefined. A leader's new power lies in his or her ability to connect, and authenticity, compassion, and alignment are the foundations for meaningful connection.

Connecting with Your Authentic Self

Becoming more authentic in your interactions with others is an important step in building connections and being compassionate, revealing your true self. The keys to authenticity are self-awareness, self-acceptance, consistency in behaviors and beliefs, and being open and truthful in your relationship with others. No one is 100 percent authentic or 100 percent inauthentic. Most of us shift from one mode to the other depending on the situation in which we find ourselves.

Think about what you do when you arrive at the office in the morning. Chances are you cover up your authentic self and don your armor—all the better to protect yourself from the slings and arrows that will soon be launched your way. Part of the problem is that high achievers often feel a burning need to be perfect. But it's this relentless focus on perfection that chips away at our humanity and authenticity. No one is perfect, after all because, you know... we're *human*.

Authenticity begins with self-awareness. You must be aware of who you are, what you believe in, how you are feeling (and what you are thinking) in this moment, and how to best express it. If you're wondering how to be more authentic in your day-to-day interactions, a good first step is to take note of how you feel in a variety of social situations. What situations make you uncomfortable—where you're breaking out in a cold sweat or determined to dash out of the room? And what situations make you feel all cozy and warm? Who do you feel most comfortable with and why? Are there certain people you work with who make you feel particularly uncomfortable? If so, what is it about their personalities that make you feel that way? What are the triggers for your inauthentic behavior, and when and where and with whom do you encounter them?

The moment you can figure out what your triggers are, you can act to avoid them. One approach to doing that is to avoid people and situations that cause you to act inauthentically. Spend more time with people around whom you feel you can be your real, unvarnished self. And then keep pushing your authenticity outward, like ripples on a pond. The more authentic you are with an ever-increasing group of people, the stronger your relationships will be. Your colleagues need to see more of *you*—the authentic you.

Research shows that authenticity is strongly associated with positive relationships, life satisfaction, a sense of purpose, self-acceptance, and well-being—all good reasons to practice it whenever you can. And in the workplace, authentic leadership is the strongest predictor of employee job satisfaction, work happiness, and low organizational turnover. So, why not give it a try?

LOOK UP, SHOW UP, STEP UP

Now that you understand the importance of connection and compassion—not just to build your Ally Mindset but to be more successful at work and at home—it's time to do something about it. Here are some proven approaches to improve your connection and compassion:

- **Start meetings with your equivalent of "Ripples and Joys."** These are brief presentations of successes participants have had and what has made them smile since you last met. Only after everyone has shared do you get down to business. The small talk really does make the big results by bringing trust to the table and building a sense of rapport and esprit de corps.

- **Schedule spontaneity and a little fun into your working relationships.** Bring your humanity to work, and you may just surprise each other. The key to this is making sure that you do it. Use status settings to signal when you are available just to chat—the digital equivalent of stopping by someone's desk. The outcome of physical distance doesn't have to be psychological distance.

- **Role-model deep presence.** How can you minimize distraction during meetings and conversations? Others know when you are paying attention and when something else has caught your attention. This has become even more apparent when we are on video calls. As they say in show business, "The camera never lies!" Stop multitasking and put all your energy and focus into the human in front of you. This alone will change the nature of your conversations and the depth and connection in your relationships.

- **Ask "How can I help?"** Don't assume that others will always share what's on their mind or ask for help. Be proactive: ask and offer. When someone does ask for help, avoid jumping to solving the issue at hand. Instead, ask what sort of help they would like. Is it empathy and compassion? Do they want feedback after you to listen to their ideas? Do they want you to tell them what to do? Or are they expecting you to solve the problem? Not all problems need to be solved in the moment; sometimes they simply need to be acknowledged.

As you have seen, connection and compassion are at the very essence of our humanity—how we show up in the presence of others. Take some time to reflect on the following questions:

- Who are the role models in your life and what do they do or not do to demonstrate connection and compassion?

- Power in relationships is being redefined with connection taking center stage. Compassion, authenticity, and alignment are crucial to connection. What are you doing in your key relationships to ensure that you are attempting to deepen connection? Do others know that you're doing it?

- Think about those people who cause you to immediately put your guard up, and ask yourself why. Is there a low-risk situation in which you could lower your wall and give it a go?

- Do people find you to be easily approachable? Why or why not? If not, identify one thing you can do to put the real you out there.

- Think about the relationship in which you feel the most com-passion. What is different about this relationship dynamic? Identify one thing that you do in that relationship that you don't do in others. Wait for the opportunity, seize the moment, and practice it with others!

- Consider saying, "Here's one thing you need to know about me that will improve our relationship." Then ask, "What's one thing I need to know about you that will improve our relationship?"

5

COURAGE AND VULNERABILITY

When You Let Your Guard
Down, the Magic Happens

66

Vulnerability is not weakness;
it's our greatest measure of courage.

BRENÉ BROWN

KEY TO DEVELOPING an Ally Mindset is having the willingness and ability to reveal ourselves completely to others, warts and all. But for many of us, this is much easier said than done. So much so that we never take the necessary step from turning intention into action. It requires having the *courage* to admit to our shortcomings and mistakes and to be open to honest and candid feedback. It also requires demonstrating *vulnerability*—owning up to our fears or concerns, asking others for help, and acting on that help when it is provided.

The good news is that being courageous and vulnerable is easier once we have forged a connection with others; we feel more comfortable and safer when we believe we aren't going to be attacked or judged if we reveal our true selves. While some think that vulnerability is a weakness, it's really a strength that can help us build relationships with others. In the case of leaders, says Paul Zak, "Asking for help is the sign of a secure leader—one who engages everyone to reach goals."

Many of us were socialized—taught by our parents, teachers, and others in our lives—to believe that being vulnerable means being weak. Vulnerable people are painted as if they're the slow antelopes at the back of the herd who get taken down and quickly become a lion's lunch. In reality, this just isn't the case. Vulnerability is where the magic happens. It takes courage to be vulnerable, and when those walls come down and one's authentic self shows up to the party, relationships really start to take off.

And we should know, because we have embraced courage and vulnerability as standard operating procedure in the work we do at SkyeTeam—both with one another and with our clients. Don't believe us? Eric is going to get all kinds of vulnerable about his struggle with some very difficult and very personal circumstances that started a couple decades ago. Here's Eric's story:

I was diagnosed with depression and anxiety in 1997, when I was twenty-six years old. I didn't know what that meant at the time. We all have our own definitions of words like these, and I was no different. I grew up in a world that didn't discuss mental health much, and when it was discussed, it wasn't pretty. My generation grew up tossing around words and phrases as playground pejoratives that we wouldn't dream of using today. Given that environment, I didn't talk about my depression. I didn't even tell my parents. It was my little secret.

Over the years, I flitted in and out of therapy, was on and off different meds, and my condition began to consume me. I still didn't talk about it with anyone. I had a lot of fear about people finding out that I was having mental problems— you can't go out and tell people that you're actually that "effed up." The internal monologue goes something like this: "You'll get fired, Eric. You'll never get another job, Eric. No one will trust you around their kids, Eric. Hell, you won't even be asked to dog sit, so sit down, shut up, and just feel better, dammit!"

About twenty years after I was first diagnosed with depression and anxiety, during the 2016 Christmas season, I lay on the floor of my office in the throes of an intense depressive episode. It was there, watching the snow fall on a tree in my yard and listening to the latest Nick Cave and the Bad Seeds record, that I planned my own death.

I said nothing to anyone. I lay there in the dark, crying.

A couple days later, I had one of those strange moments of out-of-body clarity: I knew I needed to say something to someone, I needed to get some help, or else the intention I had set in motion would play itself out. I reached out; I got myself into therapy (again). I got on medication (again), and I bought myself some time.

Then I did something odd and out of my pattern. I talked about it with my allies at work, Morag and Ruby. I don't know how much they already knew about depression and anxiety in general or if they could sense what I was going through. But I said it, and I said it out loud.

To my immense gratitude, I was met with a warm, enveloping wave of kindness and compassion. It blew my mind. To have someone tell you that you aren't broken—that's a really big deal. I was just human, going through the kinds of tough times humans go through. Morag and Ruby made it okay.

Fear of loss guides a lot of human decisions, and letting your boss and colleagues know that "your brain is broken" is a super risky proposition. Fortunately for me, they didn't judge me; they didn't cut my responsibilities; I didn't get fired.

They just hugged me.

Ever since then, I've been talking about mental health, depression, and anxiety openly. I've spoken at events and with groups about the topic. I post about it regularly.

I engage anyone who will listen. And the responses have been amazing. People reach out to me all the time to thank me for my courage. For being able to "put it all out there" and make other sufferers feel just a little more normal.

One of the most powerful comments I have received was from someone who was at the edge of the darkness, just as I had once been. And because of a post I made on the topic, they didn't kill themselves that day. So, if I can have that kind of impact on one person, just for one day, I'll talk about what I went through in every way I can, every single day.

My research shows that there's magic in vulnerability and that courage comes more readily in community. This is an experience that can make you feel utterly alone and completely lacking in worth. When you're in community, with supportive coworkers, friends, and family, you realize that you're not the first or only person to ever feel this way, and you know that your negative self-talk just isn't true. The voices inside your head can get really loud and all-consuming. It takes the perspective of someone else—someone who cares about you as a colleague, friend, or significant other—to help you reframe that.

Knowing this and experiencing this has totally changed my life personally and professionally. Because of these two amazing people in my world—Morag and Ruby—I'm still in this one.

Courage and vulnerability are inextricably linked; they go together like peanut butter and jelly, Batman and Robin, tacos and Tuesdays, and Cory and Topanga (if you get that last reference, you've just won a *very* special prize!). Courage is a human trait that has been lauded and often revered for millennia—from ancient times to today. We applaud and honor our courageous heroes. Our vulnerable heroes? Not so much. They are regularly given the label *losers*, not heroes.

Business culture often puts the bold, courageous company founder or executive up on a pedestal for all to see. There must be hundreds of thousands of articles out there written about three particularly brash business builders—Jeff Bezos, Elon Musk, and Richard Branson—highlighting their fortitude and willingness to face down the tremendous challenges they encountered as they transformed their audacious entrepreneurial ideas into reality. (Where, might we ask, are the hundreds of thousands of articles about brash *women* business builders? We're waiting...)

But do these popular ideals describe the depth of true courage? We don't think so. Courage in the context of building a business is easy; most entrepreneurs are driven to do it, courage be damned. It's the "alone in the dark" components of courage that aren't so easy; they can't be characterized by a swashbuckling hero fighting against the odds. But the courage to face those darker corners, those personal demons, is just as important as the ability to slay dragons.

Consider the example of Olympic gymnast Simone Biles and the tremendous courage and vulnerability it took for her to step back from participating in several events at the 2020 Tokyo Olympics to focus on her mental health: the peer pressure and expectations from her teammates and coaches since she was already there; the condemnation from the armchair amateurs such as Texas Deputy Attorney General Aaron Reitz who called her a "selfish, childish national embarrassment" (he later apologized); and the overwhelming pressure she put on herself as the GOAT, the greatest of all time. All this and more made her decision considerably difficult, and the courage she showed even more remarkable.

We're not all that great at doing backflips, much less the signature double layout with a half twist named in Biles's honor, and we'll guess that many of her critics aren't that great at those moves either. But now we have two good reasons to look at Biles and say to ourselves, "Wow, I wish I could do that!" whether it's a backflip or standing true to what we need for ourselves versus what others expect us to do for them.

No matter how much pressure we are under (self-inflicted or from others), having an Ally Mindset means we can choose to say no, yes, or yes if. No second-guessing ourselves or others. Simone Biles—a woman at the very pinnacle of her sport—role-modeled this in a way that few others before her have. By our definition, she didn't quit. She met the realities and challenges head-on and delivered a powerful *no*! Biles's message is one that wins all the medals in our book.

Courage and vulnerability are about not needing to win in order to win, if you get our drift. It isn't always loud and in your face; sometimes it's quiet courage. It's about knowing when to speak up and when to listen. When to move forward despite the risk and when to take a step back and reconsider. There are so many facets to this, but do it deliberately so that you and your team can nail the landing!

We ask our workshop attendees to tell us how they feel when courage and vulnerability exist in their workplaces. Here are words they use to describe it:

GROWTH MINDSET CONFIDENCE
HIGH PERFORMING OPEN
AUTHENTICITY
OKAY TO FAIL **COLLABORATION**
INNOVATION BOUNDARIES
SAFE

We all crave a lifetime
of courage. And by building
connection with others,
and inspiring them to be
vulnerable, they can
experience a lifetime
of courage.

We, of course, also ask the leaders attending our workshops how they feel when courage and vulnerability are missing in their workplaces. As you might imagine, these words are quite different:

In this chapter, we explore how courage and vulnerability work together in the Ally Mindset.

Courage: Showing Up with Your Whole Self

When we think of the word *courage*, we can't help but remember the transformation of the Cowardly Lion in *The Wizard of Oz* into a truly formidable King of the Beasts. For most of the film, the lion was filled with fear and self-doubt; he didn't believe he was courageous, and so he wasn't. It wasn't until the Wizard awarded a medal of courage to the lion, with an inspirational speech, that the lion realized he wasn't cowardly after all. The lion always had this courage within him—it was part of his DNA, part of who he was—but it took the Wizard to help him see it by bestowing upon him a Triple Cross medal.

Courage in the workplace is speaking up when you know something is wrong or when a mistake is about to be made—even if there is some personal career risk (vulnerability). A lack of feedback is an ongoing issue for leaders, and it can in fact become a career-limiting situation for those leaders if their employees don't speak up. However, there's always the danger to employees—especially in a strict, top-down, don't-call-me-I'll-call-you organizational culture—that if they speak up, that move will be career-limiting for them.

Courage is having the conviction to be true to yourself. This can sometimes be difficult. However, people may not reject you when you show them your true self. In fact, people may like you better and be compelled to build stronger, more loyal relationships with you when you show them your true self. Sure, there may be the occasional outlier, but we have found that stepping up and being courageous in the face of our fears will in almost every case get us to a better place than if we succumb to our fears and allow them to make decisions for us.

Here's an example.

A few years ago, we built a safety leadership program for a client in the oil and gas industry (or simply *petrol* for us Brits). The company had tried traditional safety programs in the past that hadn't reduced injuries to any significant degree. Eric put together a pitch for the company's top brass, and he was taken with research suggesting that a strong indicator of safety behavior was the quality and depth of the interpersonal relationships shared by coworkers at a worksite. The better the relationships, the better the safety behavior and outcomes. The intention of our program was to improve the predictability of safety behaviors in the field, leading to fewer injuries.

In an industry that has a pronounced "strength" culture dominated by men (there's a reason why they call oil-rig

drilling crew workers "roughnecks"), Eric knew that pitch-
ing a program focused squarely on getting folks in the field to
connect more on a human level was a risky endeavor. Eric's
fear was that the company leadership would react in a "We
don't do group hugs" sort of way and toss him out on his ear.
So, like all good overthinkers, he wrote up two proposals: a
touchy-feely one that truly broke new ground, and a traditional OSHA-compliant safety program that was typical for
the industry.

Just before his big pitch meeting with the company's executives in New York City, Eric had to decide. Should he go in
safe with a traditional safety program or go in bold—and
risky—with the touchy-feely, relationship-based approach,
telling the executives that their people had to start liking one
another more?

What do *you* think he decided?

After some deliberation, Eric pulled up his big-boy pants,
pinned his Triple Cross medal onto his chest (thanks, oh
great and powerful Wizard of Oz), and decided to go in big
and bold. He pitched the relationship-based safety leadership
program to the executives, and they *loved* it!

Our team went on to run the workshops for more than
one thousand participants across the country. In each workshop, fifty or so employees were coached to build and deliver
a "safety stump speech" composed of three components:
the participant's view on safety; a personal story or message related to safety; and the individual's commitments to a
safety culture, along with the commitments they were asking
of their colleagues.

As you can imagine, public speaking is not at the top of
many oil-field workers' list of favorite things to do (it's not on
the top of many people's lists—about 73 percent of the population has public speaking anxiety!) so courage was required

out of the gate. Sharing the personal stories of safety inci-
dents required talking about some very sensitive and in some
cases deeply traumatic events—big-time scares, serious injuries, and even death. In many cases, the worker who made the
error that resulted in these horrific situations was the person
telling the story and they expressed the burden of the guilt
they felt from playing a role in it.

Courage (and vulnerability!) indeed.

Says Eric about his experience during one of these workshops: "It was one of the most impactful programs I've ever
been involved in. I'm not sure I've ever seen so many big,
burly bearded dudes cry. There was rarely a dry eye in the
house at the end of these workshops; people were all in, and
the empathy was just pouring out of the room. The community building was just amazing to see."

So, all's well that ends well. Courage led us—and our
client—to the best solution, one that brought lasting change
and maybe even saved a life or two along the way. The
company experienced an 18 percent reduction in its total
recordable injury rate, which was attributed in great part to
this program. It's true: the more you know, trust, and like the
people with whom you work, the more you'll look out for their
well-being. That's true in the office, at home, or out on the
Bakken oil fields, where on a drilling platform you'll lovingly
warn your coworker that their safety glasses are still perched
on top of their head instead of over their eyes where they'll do
much more good in the event the well blows out.

When you let your guard down, the magic happens. It
takes a serious amount of both courage and vulnerability to
get there, but when we do, the results speak for themselves.

It took courage (backed up by that Triple Cross medal) for
Eric to pitch this unconventional program to the company
executives and then for our team to deliver it. And it took

courage and vulnerability for the employees to fully engage in the workshops and tell their stories. They put it all out there.

Which, now that we've mentioned it, brings us to the next piece of the oh-so-sweet Ally Mindset pie: vulnerability.

Vulnerability: Being Perfectly Imperfect

Brad D. Smith, executive chairman of Intuit, tells a story about his father, Larry Smith, who was mayor of their small hometown of Kenova, West Virginia—a real "man of the people" as Brad describes him. Brad was a young man at the time and his father was nearing the end of his life. One of the mayor's duties was to give an Independence Day speech each year, and when Brad's father gave his speech, he used the word *ain't* several times. At the time, Brad thought that to be effective, leaders needed to always appear flawless, so he pointed out these flaws in the correct use of English to his father.

Brad's father responded knowingly: "Son, people prefer their leaders with flaws, because it makes leadership more attainable for the rest of us. This is who I am, and each of them in the audience have their own opportunities to improve. But once they recognize that I can be mayor without being perfect, then maybe one of them will be inspired to be mayor after me, because they know they aren't perfect either."

Vulnerability is a willingness to put yourself into the world as you really are—to let your guard down and show up as your true, authentic self. If you're the boss, being vulnerable could be admitting to your team that you don't have the answers to a critical problem and you need their help to solve it. Or it could be making a heartfelt apology to a customer whose project didn't go according to plan. Or it could be encouraging employees to provide you with frank and candid feedback on your performance.

Being vulnerable is an uncomfortable place to be for many of us—we may feel uncertain, weak, exposed. We don't want to be wrong. We don't want others to think we don't know what we're doing. We don't want to be out of control. When we're vulnerable, we show the world that we aren't always right, that sometimes we don't know what we're doing, that occasionally we're out of control and need help.

Being vulnerable is easier for some people than it is for others, for a variety of reasons. As Mark Manson explained in a blog post: "Many of us weren't taught how to express our emotions freely. For whatever reason—maybe our home situation, maybe childhood trauma, maybe our parents didn't ever express their emotions either—we've grown up with habits embedded deeply into us to keep us stifled and bottled up."

In her book *Daring Greatly*, Brené Brown writes, "Courage starts with showing up and letting ourselves be seen." That's what we all crave—to experience a lifetime of courage and to be seen. And by building connection with others and inspiring them to be vulnerable, *they* can experience a lifetime of courage too.

Which brings us to Pizza Guy.

Just when you thought you'd heard all you were going to hear about the oil and gas industry and our unconventional safety training, here's a little heads-up: *we're back*... We have a couple more things to tell you about the people who worked for our client in the oil and gas industry.

About 70 percent of the workers who attended our workshops were 1099 independent contractors working for themselves or for other firms. This made it difficult for the company's leadership (our client) to have any direct control over them; these employees didn't report to our client's management. Yes, management could apply the stick when

The more you know,
trust, and like the people
with whom you work,
the more you'll look out
for their well-being.

it came to adhering to safety protocols on-site and not allow access, but it had created tension between crew members and impacted our client's ability to deliver their business results. Leadership felt backed into the proverbial corner, and while safety standards were largely being maintained, they weren't improving. So, getting independent contractors to do what the company wanted them to do (such as attending our safety workshops) was all about relationships.

When we conducted one of our workshops, not just the roughnecks attended. The leaders at that site would also get vulnerable and tell their own personal safety stories. This would ignite the vulnerability in the workers who attended.

Which is where Pizza Guy comes in. (Getting hungry yet?)

Picture an oil field in North Dakota in the middle of nowhere—it's a hundred miles between towns, with a liberal usage of the word *town*. The Bakken Formation straddles North Dakota, Montana, and the southern border of Canada. Our client had an operation there, and the leader of this operation (we'll call him John) lived in Texas; like all good oil people, he came from Houston. He was doing a split shift, two weeks on and two weeks off, which they called a hitch. So, John would go up to the Bakken and work for two weeks and then go home to Houston for two weeks. And when he was up in the Bakken, he didn't have anything to do when he wasn't on the job, so he decided to use that time off to find meaningful ways to connect with his workers.

John would go to the pizza joint in town and buy a stack of pizzas, put them in his truck, and drive them out to all the oil rigs scattered across his company's "play." When he rolled up to a rig, he would pull out a pizza or two, walk up to the guys working the rig, and talk with them. John told Eric, "My objective was not to talk with them about work. I'd find out about their families, kids, dogs, favorite baseball teams, whether they were Chevy or Ford guys, where they lived, and what they believed about all manner of things. Just learn their stories, who they were as people." And he became known as Pizza Guy.

Pizza Guy was a myth and a legend in the company. As we delivered workshops across the country for this client, his name kept coming up when we asked, "Who's your most awesome colleague?" Everyone just loved him.

Months later, Eric was in North Dakota doing a workshop for the oil company and John just happened to be there that week. John walked by the room where Eric was doing the workshop and popped in his head and said hello to everyone. Eric asked John if he wouldn't mind coming in to say hello. Three guys lit up when they saw him; they used to be members of John's team. One of the guys jumped out of his chair and hugged John.

Sitting at the same table was another guy, big and burly, who was obviously happy to see his former boss. John looked down at the guy sitting in his chair, and he asked, "What, I don't get a hug?"

"Aw, c'mon, you're not gonna make me do it in front of all these people are you?" asked the big, burly guy.

"I'd never make you do anything, man," said John.

The big, burly guy got up out of his chair and gave John a huge, heartfelt hug.

Eric interviewed John afterward about his leadership style.

"My leadership style is a little unorthodox," said John. That was putting it mildly.

"What do you mean by that?" asked Eric.

"I tell my folks that I love them," John replied. "They don't know what to do with that at first, but eventually they start to act similarly toward each other. That's where the magic happens. Once we hit that tipping point, my job gets really easy, because the entire team manages itself. The folks simply look out for each other and hold each other accountable."

The secret to his success as a leader wasn't that his people loved him; it was that he loved his people and he wasn't afraid to show them. He went first. He was vulnerable to the nth degree—compassionate, empathetic, and kind. Research shows that the more employees are moved by the compassion or kindness of their leaders, the more loyal they will be to them. In the roughneck culture of the oil and gas industry, saying "I love you" to your workers is being as vulnerable as you can be—sprinkled with no small amount of courage.

Five Days That Led to Fifteen Years

Before we wrap this chapter, Morag would like to get on board the vulnerability train too. She has a little secret that she hasn't told *anyone*. Here's Morag's story in her own words:

> In the US, it seems to me that being fired is often seen as a badge of honor. If you haven't been fired at least once, then you haven't tried hard enough. But growing up in England, that was not the case at all. I was brought up to believe that getting fired was a huge blot on one's career, that you were a failure, and that's the last thing you would ever talk about or reveal to others. Fear of failure (or more accurately of being judged as a failure) is one of my kryptonite weaknesses.
>
> And that's my little secret: I was fired on day five of a new job.
>
> Did I do anything that justified being fired in just five days on the job? No, I don't think so. Others tell me no. But that didn't stop my boss from walking me out on the plank and giving me a firm heave-ho off it. My fifth and final day at that company is burned deep into my mind. I was called

to a Starbucks (not the office!) by my boss, and before I could take a sip of my latte, I was told, "You don't need to come back into work. Today is your last day."

I think I experienced all the emotions possible in that moment, and off and on for several years afterward. I was mortified, perplexed, gobsmacked, embarrassed—and slightly panicked. It pulled the rug right out from under my feet. I was the sole breadwinner for my family and the thought that I had let them down and put them at risk brought me to my knees. And the idea of having to start a new job search made me feel sick with an extra dose of guilt, shame, and a side order of fear. A stress hormone cocktail was coursing through my veins, and the negative self-talk was coursing through my mind. (I said some terrible things to myself.)

However, a wellspring of determination also appeared, a vision for finally running my own business, of choosing a different career path than the one I had been on. Like a phoenix rising from the ashes of my career, SkyeTeam emerged (and yes, I can be a little dramatic). And now, fifteen years later, I've published three books and traveled the world; I'm sought out for my thought leadership; and Skye-Team continues to thrive. The icing on that delicious cake is I get to work with Ruby and Eric. None of these things would have happened but for that earth-shattering day. It turned out to be a wonderful thing.

I think that until now there were no more than five people on the planet who knew that I was fired, or let go, or however you want to describe it. Even nearly two decades later, when I think back to that meeting with my boss at Starbucks, and when I read this section in this book, I feel physically sick—all those strong feelings well up in me again.

Which brings me back to why courage and vulnerability are such important components of being an ally, of developing our Ally Mindset. In that moment of my vulnerability, I could've folded. Instead I dipped into my personal courage and took a risk to launch a business during an economic downturn. In writing this book, and finally sharing that rock I've been carrying and letting it go—allowing all subsequent successes to finally shine into that shadowy corner—I am no longer hiding from this part of my past, and I can move forward with a lighter step.

Maybe it's true what they say: the truth will set you free. Courage and vulnerability empower us to step into our truth, our lives, to connect with others in a deeper way and live our lives in full Technicolor. And who wouldn't want that?

To work, vulnerability must be honest and sincere. It's not a tactic, not a strategy, not a tool you pull out to get people to do what you want. If you're using vulnerability as a means to influence someone, you're doing it wrong. If it isn't genuine, then you aren't being truly vulnerable.

LOOK UP, SHOW UP, STEP UP

Now that you understand the importance and power of courage and vulnerability—not just for building your Ally Mindset but for being more successful at work and at home—it's time to do something about it. Here are some proven approaches to improving your courage and vulnerability:

- **Speak your truth.** When someone asks, "How are you?" how do you usually respond? Intentionally choose to tell the truth to at least one person this week when you are asked this question. Pay attention to how it shifts the depth of the conversation and how the other person responds.

- **Ask for help.** What are you really worried about right now, either from a personal or work perspective? Who can support you with a helping hand, a word of inspiration, or by being a sounding board? Reach out to them today. It takes great strength, courage, and vulnerability to share what you are most afraid of and to ask for help.

- **Explore motivation.** In your conversations with others, ask, "What excites you about the work we do? What frustrates you about the way we work together?" And, of course, be ready and willing to share your personal motivators and energy zappers too!

- **Share your story to own your story.** Much like Morag's origin story for SkyeTeam, telling your story empowers you to own your story, instead of hiding it. No mask required! Where can you share a little of your backstory, the person behind the job title, and in doing so nurture the sense of team and connection with others? We all have a story to share; we all have a story worth listening to; we all have a story that we can learn from. What's yours?

As you have seen, courage and vulnerability are at the very essence of our humanity—how we show up in the presence of others. Take some time to reflect on the following questions:

- Who are the role models in your life and what do they do or not do to demonstrate this practice of courage and vulnerability?

- What can you learn from moments in your life when, like Eric, you took a big risk and it paid off handsomely? Or like John, the Pizza Guy, when you laid it all out there and it worked out better than you expected? Keep those moments front of mind when faced with challenging workplace decisions, when the choice is play it safe or keep it real!

- In what ways are you holding back at work? Is it specific to a situation, relationship, project, team?

- What (or who) gives you courage?

- In what ways are you limiting your opportunities by playing it safe? What can you do to jump in the deep end?

6

CANDOR
AND DEBATE

Stop Dancing with the
Elephant in the Room

66

It takes a great deal of bravery to
stand up to our enemies, but
just as much to stand up to our friends.

PROFESSOR DUMBLEDORE,
Harry Potter and
the Philosopher's Stone

A S LEADERS, we are called on to speak our truth. This means having the right conversations with the right people at the right time and ensuring that these conversations are completely honest and transparent—no beating around the bush, no sugarcoating, no befogging or befuddling, no hiding behind your desk or some weirdly random Zoom background. But since the best communication is a two-way street, this also means being an active listener and fully participating in these conversations.

Whew—that's a lot.

Yes, we absolutely know that we're asking you for the sun, the moon—all that and a bag of chips too. In other words, speaking truth is much easier said than done—not just for leaders but for the people throughout the organization who work for those leaders. In fact, for someone who's not used to being candid in their conversations—to speaking their truth, the whole truth, and nothing but the truth—or who doesn't really listen to what others have to say, it can seem downright impossible. But take our word for it, the benefits are well worth any discomfort you may feel getting to this very special place.

We know. We've been there.

So, what exactly do we mean when we talk about candor and debate?

Candor is expressing your point of view in a way that increases learning and shared understanding, and it also means seeking out opportunities to both give and receive tough feedback. *Debate* is the willingness to take a stand and then explore it in discussions with others—perhaps passionately, but always respectfully. An effective debate also taps into your active listening skills. Cultivating allies is about discussing the undiscussables before they become barriers.

Together candor and debate can resolve conflict and help solve difficult business problems—by converting them into opportunities. In fact, they can do more than that. Candor and debate can dissolve conflict before it has a chance to fester and damage or destroy relationships.

But here's the rub: if you don't have candor or debate in an organization, you can end up with disengaged and unmotivated employees, many of whom will be looking for new job opportunities at places that put greater value on their opinions. In our experience, leaders set the stage for candor and debate in their organizations: when they welcome, invite, demonstrate, and expect it, others will model the behavior. When they don't, well, everything can and likely will quickly go to hell in that proverbial handbasket.

Candor happens when you have the courage to be honest about what you want, what you are thinking and feeling, and the vulnerability to share it with others, risking that it may not be received with the grace you desire. Knowing that it may be judged or ignored, or worse yet *you* may be judged or ignored. We know that being honest with others can be tough, and sometimes being honest with ourselves can be tougher still.

All of us have at some point in our lives been caught overthinking what to say and the responses we expect to receive.

As a result, we lose sight of the outcomes we are trying to achieve. We end up getting stuck and failing to say what we're really thinking, or to mean what we are saying.

Ask "How are you doing?" and the generally expected (and socially acceptable) answer is "Great!" or a solid "Fine!" An unexpected (and less socially acceptable) response is "Wow, so glad you asked, things kind of suck right now. Have you got half an hour to hear all about it? Let me tell you..."

How often have you refrained from saying what you really wanted to say, simply to keep the peace or not rock the boat? Heard that little voice in your head interrupt what you were going to say with "Don't say anything! They'll think you are [insert adjective that means you are making a mountain out of a molehill]. This isn't important. Shh... don't say anything"?

This has been Morag's modus operandi in many situations: say nothing and keep the peace. However, as we share in our emotional intelligence programs, saying nothing inevitably has consequences. As Eric often reminds us, "The philosophers known as the rock band Rush say in their research-backed hit song 'Freewill' that when you make the decision not to make a decision, then you have made your choice!" When we bottle up our feelings, when we perceive we are not valued and our opinions are not being heard, we become very unhappy, resentful people. Our silent resentment continues to simmer until it comes to a boiling point—potentially exploding into the type of brutal candor that only inflames the situation.

As Morag shares, "Even though I'm the one who chooses to stay quiet, in my mind, the prosecution is still delivering their remarks to the court (me). And unfortunately you (the defendant), who are unable to read my mind, have no idea. And so the inner turmoil continues until I choose to truly let it go. If I am not willing to speak up, then I don't get to hold a grudge; no BMWing allowed!" (That's bitching, moaning, and whining, folks, if you don't remember from earlier!)

And this inner dialogue and habit of hidden candor happens in the workplace even more frequently.

Robert was a new leader in an organization. He was super excited about making a career shift and grateful to work for this organization and have the chance to move into a new field. So, walking in the door, he was already engaged, enthusiastic, and a loyal employee; he was a high-performing rock star.

Soon after Robert arrived, the company's owner—his boss—delegated responsibility for running a piece of the business to him. There was a problem, however: the owner didn't actually give accountability for this piece of the business to Robert. He tightly held it. The boss also neglected to keep other commitments he had made to Robert.

It was clear to Robert that after only five months on the job, he was checking out—already disengaging from his work and from his organization. All the excitement and loyalty he felt when he started his new job had evaporated, and he was frustrated. When Ruby asked, "Have you told your manager how you feel?" his answer was "No, I haven't said a thing." Eventually Robert left the company for another organization where he felt more valued and where he could be his natural rock star self.

Today Robert is managing an entire business that is a direct competitor to the company he left—and he's generating stellar results. Not only did the company he left lose an amazing leader who could have bettered the way that business operated, now he's hitting them where it hurts. In the wallet and their bottom line.

Feedback is like oxygen: we need it to thrive as individual contributors. Everyone has a responsibility to give feedback, not just leaders but employees too. Robert should have spoken up and provided his boss with feedback, whether or not he asked for it. And he should have pushed the owner to provide feedback to him in return. But he didn't. And the company's owner clearly dropped the ball by not giving feedback to his employees, not asking for feedback, and for creating a culture where people didn't feel safe speaking up.

Maybe you recognize yourself in Robert's story. As Martin Luther King Jr. wrote in 1963, "The ultimate measure of a man is not where he stands in moments of comfort and convenience, but where he stands at times of challenge and controversy." All of us will be faced with moments at work and in life where we must choose to either show up and speak our truth or to shut up and allow the team to move forward despite the perceived risk.

Some examples:

- Speaking up to a toxic boss or colleague

- Challenging the status quo

- Asking tough questions when everyone else is moving to action too quickly

- Delivering tough feedback to a colleague or friend

- Having to downsize your team and let a friend go

- Pursuing a goal when others tell you it won't work

- Saying no when others are saying/expecting you to say yes

We've asked hundreds of leaders in our programs to tell us how they feel when candor and debate are a part of the places they work. Although you might have already figured out that these people feel good when they experience candor and debate at work, here are the words they use to describe it:

And on the flip side of this coin, here's how our workshop attendees feel when candor and debate are sadly not a part of their workplace culture:

EXCLUDED UNSAFE

GROUPTHINK HIERARCHICAL

DISTRUSTFUL

DISENGAGED

UNINVENTIVE

UNCOOPERATIVE STAGNANT UNTRUTHFUL

In this chapter, we'll take a close look at candor and debate and explain how you and the members of your team can use them to your advantage.

Candor: Kindly Saying What You Really Think

When you see something wrong, do you speak up? When you have a concern about a proposed decision, do you tell others? When you feel disrespected, do you let your colleagues know?

The reality for many of us is that we don't always speak up when we should. According to a *Harvard Business Review* article, research to determine if people would speak up when someone cut in line in front of them found that just one in twenty-five did. *One* in *twenty-five*! The twenty-four others stood around looking frustrated, not saying a word. They likely bitched about it later with colleagues or at home.

In addition, further research presented in the article revealed that 90 percent of nurses don't speak up to a physician when a patient's safety is at risk. Let's pause right there. Ninety percent of nurses don't speak up when (let's assume you're the patient here) your safety is at risk! On top of that, 93 percent of employees report that their organization is at risk of an accident because people don't speak up. C'mon, twenty-four in twenty-five, 90 percent, 93 percent. In many cases, lives are literally at stake! These statistics tell a compelling tale.

Long story short, a lot of people aren't speaking up at work—even people who think they are—and that sometimes puts others at risk of injury or death. Candor is a rare bird indeed.

Look up the word *candor*, and you'll find definitions along the lines of being frank, open, and honest with others. Related words include *truthful, sincere, forthright, direct, plain-spoken, blunt, straightforward, outspoken,* and so on. At its heart, candor is simply telling it like it is. The word *candor* is derived from the Latin *candere*, which means to illuminate, to shine, or to glow. When we speak with candor, we shine a light on the truth.

Cultivating allies is
about discussing
the undiscussables before
they become barriers.

Hope Timberlake, author of *Speak Up, Dammit! How to Quiet Your Fears, Polish Your Presence, and Share Your Voice*, shared her research in an episode of our *People First!* podcast: "Everybody, and I mean everybody, including me, has dealt with nervousness when speaking in front of a group of people. It's incredibly important to remind yourself of the two or three key points you want to get across. Your goal should be to channel curiosity—yours and theirs—and create the environment for the conversation that needs to happen."

But being honest, whether at home or at work, is more difficult than it sounds. We've all been on the receiving end of the corporate or personal equivalent of "Does my bum look big in this?" Damned if you do speak up and damned if you don't.

On the flip side, do we really want to work in an environment that encourages open dialogue, which if it's delivered ineloquently risks hurt feelings, embarrassment, and all the dirty laundry that truth brings with it? Politeness and candor are cousins that need to get along.

According to former General Electric chairman and CEO Jack Welch, "Lack of candor basically blocks smart ideas, fast action, and good people contributing all the stuff they've got. It's a killer." In their book *Winning*, Jack and Suzy Welch point out three specific benefits of candor:

> First and foremost, candor gets more people in the conversation, and when you get more people in the conversation, to state the obvious, you get idea rich. By that, I mean many more ideas get surfaced, discussed, pulled apart, and improved. Instead of everyone shutting down, everyone opens up and learns. Any organization—or unit or team—that brings more people and their minds into the conversation has an immediate advantage.

Second, candor generates speed. When ideas are in everyone's face, they can be debated rapidly, expanded and enhanced, and acted upon. That approach—surface, debate, improve, decide—isn't just an advantage, it's a necessity in a global marketplace. You can be sure that any upstart five-person enterprise down the street or in Shanghai or in Bangalore can move faster than you to begin with. Candor is one way to keep up.

Third, candor cuts costs—lots—although you'll never be able to put a precise number on it. Just think of how it eliminates meaningless meetings and B.S. reports that confirm what everyone already knows. Think of how candor replaces fancy PowerPoint slides and mind-numbing presentations and boring off-site conclaves with real conversations, whether they're about company strategy, a new product introduction, or someone's performance.

Candor often expresses itself as what we're thinking or feeling in our gut—the Spidey sense that something isn't right. However, candor can be career-limiting for employees in some organizations: they deliver frank but unwelcome messages upward and they are brushed aside or fired. Soon those messages will stop because employees don't feel safe delivering them. But a lack of candor can also be career-limiting for a leader. If they're not getting the warnings of impending disaster from their people, then that disaster will very likely occur, and the leader will bear the responsibility.

Candor is choosing to speak up despite the risk you may feel. It is also choosing to keep quiet because you recognize that whatever you've got on your mind won't ultimately serve the situation or the relationship. Either way, stop the BMW. Get on board and speak your truth, or get on board and withhold it. Whichever way you decide to go, be intentional, back the decision. There are no after-the-game gotchas or I could have told you so's.

It's no big surprise that Gallup has found that employees whose managers are open and approachable are more engaged: "The best managers make a concerted effort to get to know their employees and help them feel comfortable talking about any subject, whether it is work related or not. A productive workplace is one in which people feel safe—safe enough to experiment, to challenge, to share information, and to support one another."

But last time we checked, leaders aren't the only ones guilty of avoiding candor at work—far from it. Employees are often guilty of not being honest and forthright with their bosses, coworkers, customers, and others. They hide problems; they hoard information and knowledge; they're afraid to speak their minds and provide valuable feedback to others; they deceive; and sometimes they outright lie.

One way for leaders to create a culture where candor rules is to explicitly encourage and reward the behavior. Remember, you'll get more of the behavior you want from your people when you recognize it and when you role-model it. When it comes to candor, the health of your relationships matter. Adam Grant summed it up nicely: "In toxic relationships, you're forced to choose between honesty and loyalty. You bite your tongue to protect their ego. In healthy relationships, honesty is an expression of loyalty. You speak your mind to help them grow. When you have real trust and respect, candor shows care."

Don't let a lack of trust—and a resulting lack of candor—haunt *your* company or undermine your relationships.

Debate: You Can Disagree and Still Get Along

Debate is when we engage in a back-and-forth conversation with one or more people. It could be a debate among the members of an executive team about whether to lease or acquire a new office space; it could be a couple of employees trying to decide which restaurant to have lunch at; it could be a salesperson extolling the virtues of her company's products with a customer; or any number of other situations and combinations of people.

When you engage in a debate with someone, how you debate matters. Do you honor diverse voices? Are you really listening to what the other person has to say or are you too busy planning your response, so that you can pounce as soon as there's a pause? Active listening is paying close attention to the words they're saying, the nonverbal communication, and the context of the conversation. It requires deep presence. Are you really present? Are you genuinely curious and asking powerful questions? (Don't be afraid—curiosity isn't going to harm you or any cats here!) Are you trying to understand the other person's perspective? Gaining a shared understanding is critical to engaging in productive debate. Are you being empathetic?

Jordan was brought into an organization to do a turnaround; the business was underperforming, and the team needed some direction to up their game. Jordan was personable— she seemed likable enough—but when she entered the organization, she beat the hell out of the people in it.

And guess what? The employees weren't too happy about getting beat up by this outsider brought in by management specifically to kick their asses.

When Jordan completed her mission, she was given the exact same 360 feedback appraisal that everyone else on the company's leadership team went through. The feedback was predictable. While Jordan thought she was fully self-aware, amazing, wonderful—a rock star—the employee feedback was quite the opposite: You're a jerk. You're ineffective. You don't get it.

Jordan's reaction? "Well, that's obviously not me—it's their problem and I'm happy to help them work through it."

The fundamental, fatal disconnect was because of this leader's unwillingness to engage in healthy debate with her employees—it was "my way or the highway." There was in fact no debate—just proclamations from on high—and employees weren't invited to make their own suggestions. Jordan dropped candor bombs all over the organization. If employees had the courage to push back and make suggestions, the suggestions were ignored.

Jordan was given the role of turning around this underperforming organization, but she didn't look over the horizon to see that she was going to be expected to stay beyond that—to successfully run the organization long into the future. Her personal management style was all about getting short-term results and not about building long-term relationships, and this leader either wasn't able or willing to understand the gap in between.

Her relationships with employees were so damaged that Jordan exited the organization before the turnaround was complete. Her style, which had brought her success in the past, didn't work this time. She was run out of town before getting to the finish line.

There are two parts to the debate equation. The first part is hearing it: are you willing to actively listen to what others have to say and are you curious enough to engage in a back-and-forth conversation that will help you choose a new path forward? The second part is exploring it: taking the time to consider the pros and cons of the various options and then deciding to act.

According to Tiger Tyagarajan, president and CEO of global professional services firm Genpact, a healthy yet aggressive debate over issues is one of the most effective ways to come to the best decisions. But having such a debate requires that people trust (there's that word again) one another implicitly and that there is a diverse group of voices at the table. Said Tyagarajan in an interview:

> One of the things we value in our culture is debate. If you attend one of my leadership team meetings of fifteen people on a topic, such as how do we add value in the supply chain for our clients, that conversation may go on for two hours because there can be five different opinions that are debated. And when I say "debate," it's an aggressive debate—people are duking it out. But there's a lot of trust—the debate is professional, not personal. At the end of that evening, we say, "Okay, now let's go for a drink," and we celebrate the fact that I had a great debate and we've got a good answer.
>
> Debate like this really works only if you have different opinions in the room and people are willing to fight for them. You have people with different perspectives: "The sun is going to rise in the west—let me prove it to you." How do you include people who have those different opinions, and then foster a culture where people have the courage to actually speak their mind on various topics, even though they realize that ten of the people in the room have an opposite view? As a leader, you've got to foster that. If you foster that, then you get different opinions. If you get different opinions, you are able to shape better answers and better solutions. So, we've been on this journey of bringing people with different opinions into the room and creating a

culture of inclusion. And that includes people with different global backgrounds, gender—all kinds of diversity.

When we find ourselves in a candid debate that has become heated, with battle lines drawn between opposing individuals or camps, it's a sure sign that we need to take a step back from logic and focus on the emotions. Why? Because, as Liane Davey, author of *The Good Fight*, shared on LinkedIn: "Facts don't solve fights." When we lose sight of the importance of connecting with people on the other side of the debate, we stop having constructive conversations and we get stuck. And that gets us nowhere fast. Continued Davey, "Once I notice I'm in a fight, I have to remember that something deeper is going on. Fights are about values, and beliefs, and deeply held and precious notions like safety, confidence, competence, and connection. If something is making a person feel unsafe, making them feel ostracized, making them worry that they're losing control, no double-blind, randomized, empirical study is going to fix it."

Engaging in healthy candor and debate means people don't always agree. High-performing teams learn to fight well; that is, they disagree (and can do so quite vociferously). But when a decision is made, they all get behind it. Dissent happens in private—it's one voice to the rest of the organization. And more important, even after a disagreement or fight, relationships remain intact if not strengthened by the candor and debate. We can fight like hell in this room, but we go out for drinks after and toast our progress!

The Vital Role of Psychological Safety

When you're trying to encourage people to speak with candor and to engage in healthy debate—without holding back or hiding out—you've got to create an environment positively dripping with psychological safety. According to Harvard Business School professor Amy Edmondson, *psychological safety* is "a belief that it's absolutely OK—in fact, it's expected—to speak up with concerns, with questions, with ideas, with mistakes."

According to Edmondson, there are three things you can do to create a psychologically safe workplace:

1 "Frame the work as a learning problem, not an execution problem." You need everyone's brains and voices.

2 "Acknowledge your own fallibility." Say, "I may miss something. I need to hear from you." This creates more safety to speak up.

3 "Model curiosity. Ask a lot of questions." This makes it necessary for people to speak up.

Your level of responsibility for creating an environment of psychological safety (and the intentionality required to create it) exponentially increases as you move up the ladder. The further along you are in your career—as your level of responsibility and your real and perceived power increase— the less likely people will be willing to tell you the truth. To make things worse, they are also watching and assessing every move you make. The combination of the two ultimately becomes your leadership reputation and what it feels like to work on your team, whether based in truth or not.

Jesse was a leader in his industry, well respected for his technical knowledge. He had a reputation, however, for grading the work of his team members and then publicly revealing the result of these assessments to people's coworkers. Work found wanting was posted to what employees dubbed the "wall of shame," with red lines and comments.

The secret to candor
and debate is
shared understanding—
not shared agreement.

The leader's intent was to showcase what good looked like, but unlike a feel-good "wall of fame," this wall of shame created and reinforced a culture of fear in the organization. Team members spent hours planning for and revising their work before presenting it to Jesse in hopes of avoiding the inevitable critique. And indeed, like the sun rising in the east every morning, the feedback kept on coming.

When Morag met Jesse and his team on an executive retreat, the wall of shame had not been used for more than three years, yet the myths and legends about it were sticky; a culture of fear and silence remained firmly in place.

During the executive retreat, Jesse became increasingly frustrated, until he had an intensely emotional meltdown. "I'm surrounded by children!" he screamed at one point.

People squirmed in their seats, looking at one another, looking at Morag. For several minutes, no one spoke up. Senior leaders—seasoned executives with multimillion-dollar budgets—were stunned into silence. You could almost hear a pin drop.

Morag decided someone had to respond to Jesse's outrageous statement. "There are no children in this organization. There are actually laws against that," she said.

Jesse replied, "What?"

Morag repeated, "There are no children in this organization." Morag then called for a restroom break so that the tension could be defused.

She took Jesse aside, sharing the observation of what just happened: how the collective trauma of the wall of shame colored the behavior of the executive team, and how Jesse's outburst had completely mortified everyone in attendance. Jesse immediately went on the defensive. "Well, I haven't done that for years."

"That may well be true," Morag explained, "but the long shadow of your past is still being cast. It has been absorbed into the myths and legends of your organization's culture, and even new employees are planning and prepping and reworking and spending hours preparing for meetings with you for fear of getting in your crosshairs. As a result, you're not getting the messages that you need to hear."

In the end, this leader's career was undermined, despite him being so well respected in the tech community. Jesse was invited by the CEO to find other opportunities. What were the organization's executives going to do differently going forward to stand in their own truth, courage, and vulnerability to speak with candor and engage in debate? Now that the leader was gone, they had the opportunity to build a psychologically safe culture where people wouldn't be so fixated on fear of failure.

What about your organization or your team? You have the power to change a culture of silence into one of candor—even radical candor. Make it safe for people to speak their truth. Reward people for speaking their truth. Model the behavior of speaking the truth. It's up to you to take the first step. When you do, others will follow.

Are You Trapped in a Candor Bubble?

There are all sorts of examples where a lack of organizational candor and debate led directly to disastrous results—some financial, some reputational, and some deadly—including the Wells Fargo fake bank accounts fiasco, the Volkswagen diesel emissions scandal, the tragic *Challenger* and *Columbia* space shuttle crashes, and many others. The problem is that leaders often don't get the information they need from their people to nip these kinds of problems in the bud. They're trapped in a candor bubble.

So, how can you tell if you're similarly stuck? Here are nine questions that will help you find out:

1   How many barriers or organizational levels do people have to cross to talk directly with you?

2   How much of your typical workweek is spent with people outside your immediate team or function?

3   When was the last time you were dead wrong about something at work?

4   How quickly did you uncover your last mistake, and how fast did you change course?

5   How often do people ask you uncomfortable questions at work?

6   In a typical conversation, how many questions do you ask and how many statements do you make?

7   How often do you wait silently (for three seconds or more) for others to answer your questions?

8   How many times have you said "I don't know" this week?

9   When was the last time your provocative questions radically transformed part of your organization?

Leaders who break out of their candor bubble are more likely to get reliable, relevant information from their teams. In addition, they are more likely to spark the kind of debate that leads to more and better ideas being volunteered and vigorously explored by their people. The good ideas will rise to the top, and as a result, leaders can make better decisions, especially in times of crisis. Candor-savvy leaders build cultures based on mutual respect and trust.

When Feedback Hurts—Bad

Eric was facilitating a team session for a tech client—a team of software developers that had been working together for more than three years. They had a full two-day agenda planned, with a short section on feedback.

When it came time to talk about feedback, Eric asked the group to answer a simple question: How do you like to receive feedback? The answer would indicate the level of candor they wanted on their team. The team's culture was very alpha, and members routinely broke down barriers—bureaucratic, organizational, and people—to get stuff done. If someone told them no, they'd push all that much harder to prove them wrong.

The first person to answer Eric's question said, "Just tell me how it is." The next person said, "Straight between the eyes!" And with each successive person, the statements got increasingly aggressive. Someone finally said, "Smack me in the mouth with it!" Make no mistake about it, these employees weren't suggesting physical violence or a trip to the company's HR department for discipline. They were just getting all wound up in their alpha personality thing.

The last person to respond was the team's chief architect. He was sitting in his chair with his head in his hands. Finally he drew a breath and said, "Guys, if you do any of that to me, you'll *crush* me. I put so much of myself into my ideas that for you to come in here, punch me in the face, and tell me that the thing I just bled over, sweated for, and cried on for the last four months is a piece of garbage, then I don't want to talk to any of you."

In that moment, you could feel the air get sucked right out of the room—like a Dyson vacuum on steroids. Then one person on the team raised their hand and asked, "Can I change my answer?" Instead of talking about feedback for the allocated fifteen minutes, Eric and the team spent the next couple of hours talking about it. To say that people's minds were opened would be an understatement.

It's not just what we choose to say or choose not to say; it's how we say it. The secret to candor and debate is shared understanding—not shared agreement. That means that you say your piece, not just think it. And you feel heard even if we still disagree. It's this mutual respect for one another's points of view that strengthens relationships, not the kind of aggressive, inappropriate, and counterproductive candor and debate that damages relationships and causes people to sit back and shut up instead of bringing their honest opinions and suggestions to the table.

Marshall Goldsmith has a powerful exercise called feedforward, the ground rules for which help increase candor. Whether we are asking for feedback—which naturally focuses backward on the past—or ideas to solve a business issue, a natural reaction can be to critique the idea: "That will never work because..." or "We tried that in 2020, and it didn't get us anywhere." Or we immediately go to: "Yes, but..." or simply "Nope—not gonna work."

Goldsmith recommends a different approach to feedback: simply say "Thank you" and then explore the infinite variety of opportunities that can happen in the future.

We encourage you to try it next time someone offers a counter opinion or raises concerns. Instead of trying to correct the error of their ways, try:

"Thank you. Now tell me more about what brings you to that conclusion."

"Thank you. How could we modify that idea for this particular situation?"

"Thank you. What might be the unintended consequences of that action?"

By first saying "thank you" when someone presents an idea, they feel acknowledged and heard. No judgment, no grading of their suggestion. (You can also coach and mentor later, in private, if needed.) When we say "Yes, and..." instead of "Yes, but ..." we open up the possibilities and continue the conversation in a way that builds on the original idea, rather than stifling and locking it down.

Try it. You may just surprise yourself, and your team.

Using the Superpower of Candor and Debate

When you're preparing for a critical conversation with someone, have a strong sense of your purpose for the conversation or of what you need to say. Ask yourself, What is my intention for this conversation? What is the outcome I hope to achieve? Once you dig into these questions, you will either gain intense clarity on your why or why not to have the conversation.

Here are some other questions you can (and should) ask to clarify your purpose for a conversation:

- What do I want for myself?

- What do I want for others?

- What do I want for this relationship?

- How would I behave if I really wanted these results? (That is, how do I want to show up for this conversation? What is my intention?)

- How will I respond when my buttons get pushed?

- How will I respond when the other person doesn't follow the script?

- What's at risk if I don't speak up? (Not just what's at risk if I do.)

Marshall Goldsmith talks about the concept of adding too much value, and this is something to consider as you decide whether to engage in a critical conversation. Adding too much value can range from stating the obvious to repeating points just because you can (too much candor, look how smart I am) to rehashing conversations over and over (too much debate). Intent checks you at the door, with the words on the tip of your tongue. How do you, me, we move forward based on this conversation? Make an informed decision to speak up or keep quiet.

As Jack and Suzy Welch write, "To get candor, you reward it, praise it, and talk about it. You make public heroes out of people who demonstrate it. Most of all, you yourself demonstrate it in an exuberant and even exaggerated way—even when you're not the boss." You can't do this alone.

If you are the only one speaking candidly, you run the risk of living in an echo chamber. Create an environment where others don't hesitate to speak up too. Reward them when they do and encourage them when they don't. Candor and debate are vital to every organization—including your own.

LOOK UP, SHOW UP, STEP UP

Here are some ways you can role-model and gain the benefits of candor and debate in your organization:

- **Choose to speak up or let it go.** Intentionally choose to speak up and engage in the debate or turn off your unspoken (hidden) candor and move on. There is power in each of these choices, and the art is knowing when to play each one.

- **Engage in debate.** You can't just drop candor bombs and be unwilling to engage in meaningful debate. You have to be curious and hear other perspectives. Remember that fights aren't about facts; they're all about psychological safety. You're working toward shared understanding, not necessarily shared agreement. Are you being deeply present, curious, and listening when the debate starts, or do you just wanna win?

- **Create daily feedback mechanisms.** Feedback should not be saved up for a once- or twice-a-year formal performance appraisal. Feedback should be informally delivered in near-real time—as close to the event as possible. To make feedback easier to deliver, practice giving both good news and bad. Get really good at it.

- **Have regular skip-level conversations.** It's easy for leaders to only have meaningful conversations with other leaders, narrowing down their information sources in the process. This is a mistake. Seek out the truth at every level, from every employee—from the front line up. Regularly engage employees at every level of your organization, skipping your own.

As you have seen, courage and vulnerability are at the very essence of our humanity—how we show up in the presence of others. Take some time to reflect on the following questions:

- Who are the role models in your life and what do they do or not do to demonstrate candor and debate?

- In what contexts and relationships do you feel comfortable speaking your truth? Where do you hold back?

- Who on your team is the unheard voice? In which situations is your voice not heard? What other external perspectives are you missing? How will you engage them?

- How will you role-model candor and debate with others? What will you do to make it safe to speak up?

- What are your core non-negotiable beliefs and values? The ones you will fight for and defend? The more rock solid you are in your beliefs and values, the more confident you will be when supporting them.

- When things get tense, how will you respond? Be thoughtful in your response, rather than reactive. The best leaders, and the colleagues people want to work with, demonstrate emotional intelligence and respond to conflict in a confident and composed manner.

7

ACTION AND ACCOUNTABILITY

It's All Wishes, Ponies,
and Unicorns until
the Money's in the Bank

66

Do. Or do not. There is no try.

YODA,
Star Wars: The Empire
Strikes Back

CTION IS doing something, and in the context of the Ally Mindset, it is reactive in nature. It's doing what you say you're going to do when you say you'll do it. *Accountability* is proactively looking out for the needs of others. That is, you think about what they need to be successful. It's seeing what's going on around you and actively helping others. It's about the choices you make and how you show up in each of your relationships—behaving consistently, especially when in difficult conversations or times of uncertainty.

This is the capstone piece of the Ally Mindset model. It's where you take the big step beyond just talking and thinking and ruminating to doing. Everything else that we have explored in this book thus far is nothing but hot air, wishes, ponies, and unicorns. (Yes, unicorns!) It's all fantasy unless you actually do something with it and make it reality. And as you'll soon see, this is where most of us, including your intrepid authors, fall short.

We would be willing to wager that you've heard or at least read Yoda's quote from *The Empire Strikes Back* that we chose to open this chapter. The context of the quote is that grizzled Jedi master Yoda is training young Jedi upstart Luke Skywalker to use the Force to lift his crashed X-wing starfighter out of a swamp on the planet Dagobah. When a frustrated Luke says, "All right, I'll give it a try," Yoda commands, "No. Try not. Do. Or do not. There is no try."

So, to the extent that you've been surprised, blindsided, or guarded with your colleagues, it's not their fault. If you're going home at the end of the day saying, "You won't believe what happened—here's what so and so said or did," then you're having the wrong conversation with the wrong person. If you're waiting for them to take the first step, prepare for a long wait. The other person isn't the issue; you need to look inward. That's the accountability piece.

Only then should you look outward and choose how you will hold yourself accountable for acting to change the trajectory of this relationship. We all know the old saying (often misattributed to Einstein), "Insanity is doing the same thing over and over again and expecting different results."

Our advice is to avoid the insanity. This is your moment of truth. You can choose to step forward, to go first and act, or to continue to BMW (bitch, moan, and whine), while you wait and hope that someone else will step up to inspire and lead.

But if they don't, what do you get?

Nothing.

Going first is what action and accountability are all about, but like much in our work and life, it's easier said than done. Have you ever talked about changing something but never quite achieved it? Have you ever been to the gym in January? We have. Here's an example: Morag has been talking for years about getting fit. She even describes being an aspiring athlete versus a perspiring athlete in her book *Cultivate*. But despite saying it ad nauseam most every week, she continues her Olympic couch training unabated.

Every now and then, Morag will go through a well-meaning flurry of action, trying to transition from aspiring to perspiring.

Her other half recently bought a rowing machine, which is in the basement of their home. Morag began exercising a couple of times a week, but the number of weekly sessions quickly zeroed out. Zilch. Nada. She in fact recently achieved her personal best—waistline, not stroke rate.

Eric finally spoke up (putting his candor into practice): "You've been saying this for as long as I've known you, Morag. Either put up or shut up." You've got to love allies when they give you a healthy dose of candor. And he was right. We all know people who want to change but don't. We're going through the motions or emotions as we wallow in our own inertia. It's too hard, and it's not fair.

You can't motivate others to do things differently; you can only act and be accountable for yourself. We often encounter leaders who do want to change but find themselves falling back into old habits (the business equivalent of Morag's Olympic couch training), or they're unsure about first steps. They're looking for perspective on action and accountability and for advice about how to follow through.

If you're lucky, your action and accountability may ripple outward and effect change for others around you. But either way, within your personal sphere of control, how are you going to show up differently in that tough conversation with that major client, team member, or boss to move you closer to delivering your goals together?

Our friends at Acme Inc. (name changed to preserve the not-so-innocent) conducted weekly executive team meetings, as many organizations do. However, instead of really digging into issues and tackling problems, the meetings had become routine, boring readouts—theaters of collaboration. Each department head would duly report in, saying, "This is what's going on, nothing much," and that was it. All surface-level stuff. There was the appearance of harmony and alignment on the surface, because everyone was super nice and polite with one another. But beneath the surface, there were deep currents of smoldering resentment.

The same three people always talked first and carried the conversation. They embraced candor and debate, but they were the only ones doing it. The other five people on the team just sat back and stopped sharing because when they had tried, they were shut down before they even finished their thoughts. As a result, these meetings turned into marathon ordeals where nothing much happened, and nothing ever changed. The executives were nice to one another in the room and snarky behind one another's backs.

On the one hand, where it got really toxic was with the talkative ones, the individuals who dominated the conversation. They just assumed agreement and tacit compliance from everybody else. And then they were surprised when they were later blindsided and things didn't go the way they thought they would go, or results were underwhelming.

The quiet ones, on the other hand, were frustrated that they never got the opportunity to feel heard or validated. This is a concept of learned helplessness that lowers the bar of performance, and certainly the ability to react and deal with issues, challenges, or even new opportunities. There was neither action nor accountability; the team was just stuck. So stuck that in a decision that when we got together with them more than a year later, they still had not communicated the decision to employees, or rolled out the required new processes. As a result, customer retention was waning and this company was even further behind competitors in adapting to the realities of their changing industry. While we like to think we can make magic everywhere we go with our clients, sometimes old habits are so entrenched that no amount of cajoling from our side can move the needle.

Here are words associated with action and accountability in organizations:

And here's what it looks like when action and accountability are missing:

Action is the view from the outside in. It is your impact. Accountability is looking from the inside out, driven by who you want to be.

Action is the view from the outside in. It is your impact, what people see and judge you on. Accountability is looking from the inside out, driven by who you want to be, informed by abundance and generosity from your base values. But keep in mind that these two elements must be in balance. If you have all action without accountability and haven't invested in connection and compassion, you're the brilliant jerk. And if you have all accountability without action, perhaps coupled with high candor and debate, then you may talk a good game but end up taking on too much to save the day—at risk of dividing the team, creating a victim or passive culture, and personally burning out.

Stephanie was recruited to lead the finance organization for her business. She's a hard driver. Stephanie arrived with clear ideas on what needed to be changed, including new systems and new approvals. Over the course of a year, she drew many lines in the sand and kept her peers and other leaders at arm's length. Her attitude reeked of "I'm the expert; I came from an Ivy League school. I've got this." Despite her long résumé, achievements, and yes, her Ivy League credentials, her peers on the leadership team were making a sport of avoiding her. They didn't see her as a go-to leader or a resource they could rely on or trust. Finance was becoming a silo and a drag on the entire business.

Even within her own team, there were rumbles of discontent. The members of Stephanie's team didn't want to approach her because she barked orders, interrupted, and did not listen. Half the time she gave someone a job to do, she ended up butting in and doing it herself. She was anything but empowering; she didn't provide the team with the support they needed to learn and step up.

The leadership team had a meeting during which Stephanie presented a solution to a big client-billing issue. In true

Stephanie fashion, she was arrogant, dismissive, and used technical terms and jargon that left everyone more confused than when she started her presentation. When asked clarifying questions by others on the leadership team, to say she "bit their head off" was not hyperbole.

Stephanie was all action with no accountability—at best a brilliant jerk. But in reality she was perceived by others as just a big jerk.

So, what gets in the way of action and accountability? It's most often because in many organizations, teams, and other relationships, there's a thin veneer of politeness over a thick layer of apathy. This drives truth-telling underground and increases the chatter on the watercooler Slack channel after meetings. (You have one of those, don't you?)

But it doesn't have to be that way. In this chapter, we'll consider this essential practice—action and accountability—and how to put it to good use for yourself and for your organization.

Action: To Step Into Doing

Action—doing something instead of just talking about it—goes back to the Four Yeses questions that we introduced in chapter 4. It captures the essence of the first question, Can I count on you? This question is all about credibility. Do you do what you say you're going to do? Do you keep your commitments? Do you renegotiate when you can't? Renegotiating requires vulnerability. You have to let the walls down and be accountable. You have to admit that you missed the mark and couldn't do what you thought you could, and you cut a new deal.

Most busy people are constantly prioritizing life and work commitments—acting on some of them and then rationalizing others away. Action is reactive in nature because it means you're keeping your word. You're following through on a commitment, and you're *intentionally* choosing to do so on time and at the level of quality that you promised.

We have long been inspired by a simple concept in *The Leadership Challenge*, written by James Kouzes and Barry Posner. According to Kouzes and Posner, "If you don't believe the messenger, you won't believe the message." To be believable and to gain the trust of others, you must (in the authors' acronym-centric lingo) DWYSYWD—that is, you must *do what you say you will do*. If you don't follow up your words with action, why would anyone believe you? (Here's a hint: they won't.) When you keep your commitments, this creates an opportunity for others to feel heard—and that is a major foundation for building trust.

Action is about showing up—being present in the moment, in the meeting, in the conversation. You don't bury your head in your computer, absentmindedly send texts, check the latest price for bitcoin, or allow other distractions to interfere. Your actions speak louder than words.

Not keeping commitments can breed stagnation. Action is moving forward, accomplishing your goals. If the overall effort is overwhelming, you can break it down into smaller pieces or steps that are easier to control and accomplish.

This goes for teams as well, not just individuals. High-performing teams have an uncommon discipline to do what they say they are going to do. They create a clear, common, and meaningful purpose—why the team works together—and they conduct effective meetings (that start and finish on time) with clear purpose (to discuss, to decide, and so on) and with the right people in the room (and by that we don't mean *everyone*). They create an action plan that ensures they execute their goals and hold each other accountable for expectations and standards. In addition, they reward and celebrate both team and individual successes, and most important, they have fun.

Accountability: To Serve and Support

Accountability is proactively looking out for opportunities to serve and support others. (Think servant leadership here.) Accountability is also ensuring that you serve and support your own needs and goals. Not one or other in isolation; it is both sets of perspectives and needs in alignment. If you've ever heard yourself saying yes as you're thinking, "There's no way I have time for that," then you know what it feels like when accountability for yourself is out of alignment with your desire to be accountable to others.

It's not just about your actions; accountability is also about *how* you do those actions. Like action, it relates to the Four Yeses, in this case the second question, Can I depend on you? It's seeing an issue and owning its resolution— proactively removing obstacles and making others' lives easier, more enriched, and lighter. In the Ally Mindset, you want to be clear that if something doesn't serve you, you reserve the right to say no. If by saying yes you put at risk your other projects, stress level, or workload, it's much better to say no graciously than to take on too much.

It all sounds so easy. But we know how hard it can be to say no to requests from others. However, a gracious "No, not today; how about tomorrow?" or "How can we reprioritize my other projects?" goes a long way to ensure that everyone's needs are considered, and to agree on an informed way forward together. When we don't share our inner no and we simply say yes, it's too easy to find ourselves seething with resentment and undermining ourselves in the process. This is where we come full circle: action and accountability connect back to abundance and generosity, and to the guardrails we identified at the start of this book.

In just a handful of words, Brené Brown demonstrates the interconnectedness of all the Ally Mindset concepts we've shared with you in this book: "Generosity cannot exist without boundaries, and we are not comfortable setting boundaries. Because we care more about what people will think and we don't want to disappoint anyone, we want everyone to like us. And boundaries are not easy. But I think they are the key to self-love and I think they are the key to treating others with love and kindness."

As you may have gathered, accountability is the more proactive element in the action and accountability pairing. It's how you show up, regardless of whatever else is on your calendar, regardless of whatever commitments you might have made or not made. It's about looking up from your work and looking out to seek opportunities to help others around you, and yourself.

Accountability is not just about taking the blame when something goes wrong, which is what people often think. There's always that one person on the team who says "I'm really sorry" when things go wrong, even though it wasn't their fault. They had nothing to do with it. That's not accountability; that's just taking a beating that you don't need to take. But societally we've come to conflate accountability with taking the blame.

One of our client's organizations has a very aggressive, type-A culture. When talking about how to increase accountability throughout the company, they used the phrase "one throat to choke." (Fortunately, it wasn't our throat!) The idea was that for each decision made, one person owned it—the one throat to choke.

While clarity of roles and responsibility is important, this isn't accountability. Accountability is owning the successes and the mistakes. It's about delivering on your commitments, organizationally and personally. It's accountability for the outcome, not just the tasks, which is an important distinction. Accountability, like leadership, happens at all levels and it's necessary everywhere. You don't have to be a manager or a leader to be accountable for something in your organization.

Sometimes you must hold yourself accountable because you are the only voice in a decision. But there are times when other people are in the mix and you're going to have some tough conversations—either about their accountability or your own. This is true ownership.

The key is realizing that you must take that responsibility. Because when you're personally accountable, when you own those situations, you see them through. You're going to finish the job, whether it's good or bad. And you don't blame others when things fall apart or go down in flames. You just do your best to make it better.

But this is all predicated on building strong, trusting relationships. Relationships and reputations are built or destroyed one conversation at a time. Every conversation, every day is a fresh start. Don't dwell on the shoulda, coulda, woulda. Forgive. Learn. Move forward.

Here are three relationship pulse check questions that you should ask to determine personal accountability:

1 What is working?
2 What is not working?
3 What is one thing I can do to ensure my/your/our success?

This is your moment
of truth. You can choose
to step forward,
to go first and act.

If you take away nothing else from this book, do use the relationship pulse check. It's one of the easiest things you can do to promote accountability, and it's an opportunity to go first and show up like an ally. These questions demonstrate commitment and accountability for the relationship and a willingness to act and do something differently. Do people feel safe, trusted, and empowered around you, or do they feel diminished, hesitant, and guarded?

In *Cultivate*, Morag shares the story of Anne, a boss from early in her career who micromanaged her people and took credit for everyone's successes. This had a negative impact on Morag's and her coworkers' engagement. Was Anne wrong? Sure, her leadership style was not one that encouraged people to give their best. At the same time, however, Morag didn't take accountability for asking what was driving Anne's behavior or what she needed. There was no trust, no psychological safety, no connection and compassion, no courage and vulnerability, no candor and debate from either of them. Morag and Anne both suffered as a result.

Managers and executives high on the org chart can't expect those who report to them to be accountable unless they role-model the behaviors and follow through on their commitments. Walk the talk. Don't just talk the talk.

Action is about applying uncommon discipline and keeping commitments on your team, while accountability is going the extra step—recognizing a coaching moment, pausing, and doing the right thing instead of the simple or fast thing. This goes even beyond your commitments to the work and to each other. Sometimes it's that extra little note of gratitude or picking up of someone's work to support them.

This is the secret sauce to building teams: doing something unexpected helps strengthen relationships, as well as the team's performance.

Action and Accountability:
The Capstone of the Ally Mindset

As we explained at the beginning of this chapter, without the capstone of action and accountability, the other components of the Ally Mindset don't add up to much.

The Ally Mindset is all about inspiring, aligning, and delivering. When you have people who aren't performing or who are bad actors, you need to deal with them directly—not just ignore them or sit them in a corner. Many companies deal with underperformers by taking them out of their teams and putting them on "special" projects where they can work indefinitely with no consequences—marginalized and not a part of the organization's mainstream.

However, some "nice" cultures are anxious about holding people accountable—as if it's a bad thing. They tend to believe that you can either be nice or you can hold someone accountable, and you can't do both. Holding people accountable has this negative social implication of being mean or tough, but that's not the case or the intention at all. If you show up as an ally, when you give tough feedback and hold someone accountable early in the game, this prevents them from failing in a bigger, more substantial way later.

Organizational psychologist Adam Grant shared on Twitter some thoughts pertinent to action and accountability: "When people overstep, it's not always because they don't respect your boundaries. Often it's because you haven't drawn your boundaries. If you don't tell them where the line is, how can they learn to stop crossing it?"

Personal action and accountability aren't just about your intentions; they're about the results. But action without alignment and grounding in your values—and *our* shared vision—creates chaos and disconnection. Ask yourself, What do I need to do to reconnect with compassion, to reclarify expectations, to demonstrate courage and vulnerability, and to admit "You know what? I messed up"? Having an Ally Mindset doesn't guarantee success, but it does increase your chances of success *together*.

We're all human and having an Ally Mindset will not make you perfect, nor will it guarantee that you effortlessly navigate all the difficult situations in life.

You're going to mess up and make mistakes.

You're going to blow it. Sometimes spectacularly.

When you inevitably miss the mark, whether by your own definition or by others', you need to think rationally and remain objective. You need to act toward others in a way that builds understanding, connection, and success. Nurturing your Ally Mindset isn't just about striving for success; it also informs how you recover from your missteps along the way.

When someone makes a mistake, instead of throwing up your hands in horror or despair or berating someone (or yourself—think about the insidious little voice in your head), lean on the elements of an Ally Mindset. Here's an example of how the different components of the Ally Mindset build one on the other, when you need to give or receive feedback:

- **Abundance and generosity.** This is the starting point, the foundation that sets up the other components that follow. When someone makes a mistake, you give them the benefit of the doubt that they didn't do it on purpose. By providing feedback you help prevent future mistakes while increasing the opportunity for your colleague's future success.

- **Connection and compassion.** Empathy and heart-led caring is critical. Give your colleague the feedback they need to hear—empathetically, in a way they can hear it—not just the feedback they want to hear. Check in first: "Is now a good time to share some feedback?" If not, schedule a later conversation.

- **Courage and vulnerability.** With your authentic self fully available, provide feedback that needs to be heard, especially if it's a tough message to give or there's a risk for them or for you. You're willing to take this personal risk to ensure your colleague's personal success.

- **Candor and debate.** If you're authentic, you can say what needs to be said, in a two-way conversation that includes the other person and not in a one-way monologue. Instead of "You messed up, go fix it," the message is "What was your experience? How might we step forward together?" You stay curious so that understanding and learning can follow.

- **Action and accountability.** Once you have agreed on a path, you must walk the talk, act, and be accountable to yourself and others. Own your promises and follow through on them—building trust in the process.

So, whether you're giving or receiving feedback, the Ally Mindset wins hands down. It creates a constructive, increasingly positive momentum—a rising tide that raises all boats, not a destructive or negative drag to the bottom, one that may scuttle the boat. With an Ally Mindset, in an ally relationship, the feedback may still sting, but we love you for providing it. We are better because of it. The alternative, when feedback is withheld, means we get blindsided—"Why didn't you tell me that six months ago?"

The Ally Mindset is about intentionality, about conscious choices. *Your conscious choices.* Speak up or don't, do or don't. But if you choose the latter, you can't then secretly hold

The Ally Mindset is all
about inspiring, aligning,
and delivering.

that thing against a person, because they don't even know about it.

A quote attributed to Peter Drucker gets to the heart of this: "Only three things happen naturally in organizations—friction, confusion, and underperformance. Everything else requires leadership." And that includes the quality of your relationships and your reputation and impact. The Ally Mindset sets the stage for choosing how you look up, show up, and step up in your relationships:

- **Look up.** How do you want others to feel in your presence?

- **Show up.** Are you intentional about how you're showing up? (For example, turning up the dial on candor when your voice needs to be heard.)

- **Step up.** Are you doing your best? This is where the rubber meets the road, and action and accountability come into their own. Reflect every day on what worked, what didn't work, and then pick one thing you can do tomorrow to improve your game.

Ultimately, the practice of action and accountability builds trust. People who embrace this practice care about follow-through; they care about keeping promises and meeting deadlines; they care about telling it like it is. Trust is built when people can count on you to do what you say you'll do and to finish what you start. Trust is eroded by failing to do these things.

Like the other four practices, action and accountability can be overused or underdone. Ruby experienced a situation early in her career where she overplayed action and accountability while missing the other parts of the Ally Mindset. Explains Ruby:

In the 1990s, I was a project manager leading a global team at Seagate, and I had team members in Asia, the US, and Europe. We were launching a global survey to over forty thousand people, and there were tons of logistics involved. We had several languages to translate. Some people had computer access, some didn't. It was a super complex project to roll out, and my role was to get the global HR community aligned on implementing it.

I was well known in the organization for being a task-master. That's why I was in charge, right? I was really good at it, very efficient. So efficient that when people came into my office at that time in my career, I would sometimes act like I was on the phone or I would stand up and pretend I was going to a meeting, because I didn't want to take ten minutes to talk to them. I was like, "Get out of here. I got things to do!"

But one day I realized I didn't have allies on my team. I got a call from the VP of HR in Singapore. At that point in my career, I had no business getting a phone call from someone at that high level in the organization from across the world. He was really upset about a decision we had made in a meeting. In that conference call, I had checked in with each team member to make sure we were all in agreement. Not one person spoke up. And then they went away and told their boss, who ended up calling me, creating a lot of issues and anxiety for all.

After speaking with the VP from Singapore, I realized that the team didn't want to disagree with me because they knew I just wanted to get the work done. I wanted to efficiently make the decision, complete the project, and move on. I was too focused on business results and not focused enough on building connection and encouraging candor and debate. My meetings were very agenda driven, pushing to get through all the points and end on time, leaving no time for people to speak and be vulnerable and courageous, especially in that global context.

At that moment, I realized that I had no allies on the team. I was alone, and if I wanted things to change, it would have to start with me.

Ruby's story reinforces the fact that the five practices of the Ally Mindset don't function well in isolation. They connect and build on each other. If you're only doing some of them, then you are going to be falling short for yourself and falling short for others. To put the Ally Mindset to work, start with yourself first, then work outward to others.

Take the first step. Model the behavior. Build trust. Be an ally. Others will follow your example. Trust us, they will.

LOOK UP, SHOW UP, STEP UP

When it comes to action and accountability, every one of us can do a bit better, try a little harder, and accomplish better outcomes. If you would like to improve how you show up in this practice, here are some recommendations:

- **Practice consistent self-reflection.** This is not self-judgment but rather a constant focus on being your best. This also comes with grace: know that your best will look different every day, depending on what else is going on in the world around you (and/or inside your head). Complete a daily reflection on these three questions: How do you want others to feel in your presence? Are you being intentional about how you're showing up? Are you doing your best?

- **Take responsibility for the health of your professional relationships.** This is about proactively assessing the quality of your relationships, building connection, and making them stronger. Reach out to team members and take a pulse check. Ask them, What is working in this relationship? What is not working? What is one thing I can do to ensure my/your/our success?

- **Do or do not, there is no try.** Taking action is best explained by Jedi master Yoda. If you don't act first, you can't be an ally. Are you leaning in to the actions that you need to take?

Action and accountability are the capstone of the Ally Mindset—they provide the spark that makes all the other components of our model work together in harmony. Take some time to reflect on the following questions to see if this practice is the capstone of your working style:

- Who are the role models in your life and what do they do or not do to demonstrate action and accountability?

- What's one thing you can do today to get uncomfortable and step into taking accountability?

- What problems or challenges are impacting you that need to be addressed? What opportunities are waiting for you to leverage? Which are within your control and/or influence? Which are you ready and willing to act on?

- In what contexts or relationships is it easiest to take action and accountability? On the flip side, where is it harder for you to keep your commitments and really show up for others?

- What commitments have you missed? In which relationships might you need a cleanup conversation?

8

FROM ADVERSARY TO ALLY

Even Darth Vader
Left the Dark Side

66

The best way to destroy
an enemy is to make him a friend.

ABRAHAM LINCOLN

I N THE FIRST CHAPTER of this book, we told the story of how Robin was more than just a sidekick to Batman—he was his closest ally and best friend at work. And while Batman and Robin were out fighting crime (Holy bat signal!), Bruce Wayne's valet, Alfred, took care of business at home— allowing Batman and Robin to be who they really were. All three of these comic-book characters had each other's backs: supporting one another when they needed support and cheering each other on when they needed a stiff kick in the rear end.

Who has your back, and whose back do you have?

We all know (some of us all too well) that business is a competition for limited resources: everything from people to money to mindshare to any number of other things. However, while the Ally Mindset is based on the idea that there are plenty of opportunities for everyone—and by working together as allies, instead of working against each other as enemies, we can all achieve so much more—there will be times when your intent is not understood, and your impact is misinterpreted. There will be times when others might misperceive you as a rival or adversary.

When your words and actions don't align, it damages your reputation and your career. And if you're in a leadership role, this gap could also be hurting your company. While you may think you're a misunderstood genius, keep in mind that your misunderstood genius is someone else's brilliant jerk.

In this chapter, we'll reveal the secret to coming back from career missteps and repairing the damage to your reputation and relationships—turning rivals and adversaries into allies who can help you achieve your goals, as you help them achieve theirs. As we move forward, keep in mind the immortal words of American author, salesman, and motivational speaker Zig Ziglar: "You will get all you want in life if you help enough other people get what they want." There's a ton and a half of wisdom in those eighteen words.

What's Your Number?

On a scale of one to ten, with one meaning "everything sucks," and ten is "I am jumping out of my skin happy," what's your number?

Morag was recently coaching a senior leader in the tech industry, and she started each coaching conversation by asking "What's your number?" The leader's organization is a little chaotic and it's been getting worse since the pandemic. Shifting into work-from-home mode just made everything even more fractured. When Morag asked this leader, "What's your number?" the answer was three out of ten.

Think about that for a moment: three out of ten. It sucks. In September 2021, McKinsey reported that nineteen million American workers had quit their jobs since April 2021, a record pace that is "disrupting businesses everywhere." Not only that, but McKinsey also reported that 40 percent of employees are likely to leave their current job in the next three to six months. And of those 40 percent of people who are likely to leave their current job in the next three to six months, 64 percent said they will leave without another job already lined up.

The Great Resignation was in the headlines everywhere in 2021, and research like McKinsey's shows just how bad things got. Quitting isn't new; staff turnover isn't new. What was new was the pace of change, and that employees were no longer willing to tolerate (brilliant) jerks or bad coworkers. Relationship health matters. Whether or not the Great Resignation becomes a footnote in the long history of work, retaining talented leaders and attracting talented employees remain core to the people strategy of many organizations. Indeed, at the heart of most people's career strategy is finding a great place to work, where they can thrive, grow, and add value. So, the question is, How do you flip the paradigm of the Great Resignation on its head and turn it into the Great Attraction?

Everything you do to fill the relationship bucket for you and for your colleagues matters. It's the difference between "I quit" and "I fit." Again, going back to that McKinsey research, having a sense of belonging, being valued by their manager and their organization, and having caring and trusting teammates were most important to employees. McKinsey found that these qualities were more important to employees than employers appreciate; they are being overlooked by employers and, as a result, are key reasons why employees are leaving their companies.

Organizations tend to focus on less relational factors, such as "We're not paying people enough" or "We're not giving them enough flexibility" or "We're not giving employees enough health benefits." What's really fascinating about this gap in priorities between employees and employers is that if you focus on human connections, which have a budgetary cost of zero, then you don't have to worry so much about whether you are paying people enough, giving them the flexibility they need, or providing enough benefits.

When people feel checked in and engaged and they have some best friends at work, they feel good about where they're at—their number will more likely be a seven, eight, nine, maybe even a ten. Even if it drops to a three, they know that the down period will likely be short lived, and that their teammates will support them through it. And they're much less likely to be looking for another gig. People tend to job search when they lack what they consider to be most important at work—the relational elements. They want to be seen and know they matter.

Now if you as a leader or an organization shake more money at an unhappy employee to entice them to ignore the voice in their head and stay, that's great, but it doesn't solve the problem. It just buys you a little time as you kick the can further down the road. And how much more time is that money going to buy you? How long will it take before that employee doesn't feel a sense of belonging, doesn't feel valued, and doesn't have the care or trust of their teammates? That extra money is going to raise the employee's standard of living by some nominal amount, but the underlying problems have not changed. For them, it will still fundamentally *feel* the same.

We know when relationships are going well. We can identify that. We also know when they're going off the rails. It's when we leave work at the end of the day, or we sign off Zoom, and we say to others, "You won't believe what happened today at work." And we dread going back in the morning.

What's your number?

Writing Stories

In the last four weeks, have you ever found yourself saying yes when you actually meant no? You didn't want to let others down, but that might have led you to overcommit. We saw that happen a lot during the pandemic, especially when work and family commitments weren't as visible to others. Or you might have stayed silent to protect people's feelings, but in reality you stopped telling the whole truth and nothing but the truth. Or have you said "I'm fine" when you were feeling overwhelmed and on the edge of burnout, being "professional" to the bitter end?

If so, welcome to the club.

The fundamental problem with this approach is that it creates a huge gap between our intention and our impact. We judge ourselves by our intent because we know what we mean, what we're trying to accomplish, and what we're capable of. But everyone else judges us by how what we do lands—and we them. Saying one thing but feeling another has a huge influence on the quality of our working relationships because we write stories about each other. And we don't talk about it. Why not? Because we write stories about the stories, or at least stories about how someone might react if we do raise the subject. If you're like us, you've probably run unspoken stories (excuses) like these through your mind more than once or twice—and as a result not spoken up:

- If I share my thoughts, you'll get mad at me, and that would be harder than what I have to share

- If I tell you, you'll get mad at me, and I just don't have the time or energy for the argument

- If I tell you, you'll deny it or tell me it's all in my mind

- I'm supposed to know this, or do this, so you'll think I'm incompetent

- I don't want to hurt your feelings

- This has been going on for too long; I can't raise it now

But talking about the stories we may be writing, before they become epic sagas, is the core component to moving a relationship toward ally status. It's what we call *making the implicit explicit*. You could also call it *contracting the obvious*. These are all the little idiosyncratic things about relationships that we take for granted. They don't happen magically; they happen if we're lucky. If we happen to be on the same page or wired the same way, great, but that's leaving a lot up to chance. And as the familiar saying goes, "Hope is not a strategy." We all write stories about each other and assume people think like we do.

Morag recently started to write an epic story, one based on assumptions, not facts. Here's what happened:

I recently texted a colleague and realized after a few days that I hadn't heard back. I assumed he was busy.

I sent another message—still no reply. At that point, my mind started to go into overdrive. Did I have the wrong number? No. Is he mad at me? He's usually responsive, so perhaps. Something must be wrong. Maybe it's me. I must have done something that annoyed him. But what? He's mad at me because I haven't called him, but he hasn't called me either.

And, of course, every time I see him post on social media or LinkedIn, the stories I'm writing become even more personal. He has time for Instagram but not for me. I must have really goofed.

When your words and
actions don't align, it
damages your reputation
and your career.

When we're trying to assess where relationships are and what choices we have in them, we often operate in this place of imperfect information. Show us a place—any place—today where we have perfect information. We just don't. The more imperfect the information that we have, and the more left to our own devices we are, the more often the endings we write to those stories tend to have two characteristics: they're personal and negative.

Morag continues:

> So, I took a deep breath and I tried again. And still crickets.
> A few days later, I finally got the message that I had been waiting for. Turns out he'd been navigating a whole lot of stuff at work, at home, in life, which culminated in an accident that broke a bone in his foot. It was nothing to do with me. Never was. And it certainly wasn't because I had done something wrong.
> We spent a great couple of hours on the phone and put the world to rights. We picked up right where we left off, excluding my little off-road mental adventure.

What Morag experienced happens at work all the time. Let's imagine for a moment that you have a colleague who is a habitual interrupter. They've just cut you off mid-sentence— again. What stories are going through your mind as your colleague does that? What do you tell yourself about that colleague?

When Eric first started working with Morag, he found himself in this very situation:

> Every time I would bring up an idea or have a thought about something, I would get about 20 percent into whatever I had to say, and Morag would go, "Ooh... let me tell you

about this." And she would "Arnold Horshack" (this is a reference to a 1970s sitcom—YouTube it, you'll laugh) her way into the conversation.

And I'd be like, "What's going on here?" and I started writing stories. The stories I wrote were "She doesn't want to hear what I have to say"; "She doesn't care"; "She wants to hear herself talk"; "She thinks her ideas are better." So, I started to shut down and I didn't contribute anything.

Ruby noticed what was going on and asked me about it. And I was like, "Well, Morag doesn't care what I have to say. We're just going to do whatever she wants to do. So, why should I even waste my time?"

Ruby made us talk about it, and when I put my feelings on the table, Morag was horrified. She said, "Oh my God, no. When you start talking, I get excited, and I want to hear more about the idea you just shared. We can come back to what you were about to say later!" And I responded, "Yeah, I get it, that may be your intention, but wow, that is not how it lands on me."

So, it's funny. She didn't do it to be rude. She didn't do it because she wasn't interested in my suggestions and opinions. She kept jumping in because she was truly interested in what I had to say.

Eric's story reminds us that we get choices in how we show up. What can we do to show up differently, to (in Morag's case) listen just a little bit longer? The stories we write will either keep us trapped or they will empower us. In Eric's experience, he was trapped for months until Ruby forced the issue, and he and Morag broke through the bad habits that had defined their relationship up to that point.

Have you ever felt as if you were trapped in someone else's point of view about you—and you were misperceived or misunderstood? You see yourself as caring and committed, but they see you as a micromanager. And have you ever trapped someone else in your own point of view? You see the person as stubborn and difficult, but the person wants you to see persistence and dedication.

What are the stories about you when you're trapped in other people's points of view? And what impact have those perceptions had on your leadership, your ability, your reputation, your relationships?

To mind the gap, you must be conscious of the gap—the difference between people's stories, including your own, and reality. And remember, 67 percent of people who completed the Ally Mindset Profile indicated that their success has been undermined by a colleague. That's two in three leaders, which implies, odds on, that you are the one undermining others (much like Morag with Eric) without realizing it.

When things don't go according to plan, when others don't respond as anticipated, we tell ourselves personal and negative stories to explain the situation. Being an ally requires us to remain curious, give the benefit of the doubt, and assume positive intent—whether that's for others or for ourselves. Write positive stories as well as negative ones when the situation warrants it.

Think about these gaps and talk them through with others around you. It's essential when you're deciding what needs to be done about an individual relationship, as with Eric and Morag. It requires being vulnerable. And that can be scary depending on the intensity and negativity of the stories we've written about a misperception or misunderstanding. But here's what we know: the chances of you breaking out of these stories on your own are slim at best.

Get Real

When we ask people to describe what an ally is, they invariably can create a long list of synonyms quite easily. Words like *friend*, *supporter*, *colleague*, *helper*, *accomplice*, and on and on. What words would you use to describe what an ally is?

Think about three people who have had a major impact on you and your career. How does your description of an ally line up with each of these people? The difficult part of being an ally is not a lack of knowledge about what we should do; we know what ally relationships look like. The difficult part is being consistently intentional and following through with the required actions. And that goes from the very top of most every organization on the planet right down to the frontline, minimum-wage worker. It takes uncommon discipline to do this stuff.

How do you think most leaders show up? As allies who win the undying loyalty of their people or something less than that? Perhaps it's no big surprise that research shows most people find their managers to be somewhere south of ideal. Recall the results of a 2020 McKinsey survey we cited in chapter 2: over half of American workers claim their boss is mildly or highly toxic. And if that wasn't bad enough, three-quarters of American workers say that their boss is the most stressful part of their workday.

Where did all those allies go—the bosses as friends, supporters, colleagues, helpers, and so on? Guess what? You are the mildly to highly toxic person to someone in your organization. It doesn't matter if you're an executive, manager, supervisor, formal or informal leader. You are someone's most stressful part of their workday. How would your people— the individuals who work for you—rate you on the toxicity

Your misunderstood genius is someone else's brilliant jerk.

scale? How many of your people would cite you as the most stressful part of their workday?

When you spark conversations about how we show up at work, and when we try to realign and reset a relationship, chances are you're going to get feedback. Being an ally means you're going to get the feedback you need to hear before it becomes career-limiting. And sometimes that feedback isn't warm and cuddly; it can be rough and tough, and it can sting. As a human being, one of your first reactions will likely be to justify and negate the feedback you receive from others.

Peter Bregman is a colleague of Morag's in Marshall Goldsmith's 100 Coaches organization. In a *Harvard Business Review* article, Bregman describes thirteen ways that we defend ourselves from negative feedback that threatens our self-perception:

Play Victim: "Yes, that's true, but it's not my fault."

Take Pride: "Yes, that's true, but it's a good thing."

Minimize: "It's really not such a big deal."

Deny: "I don't do that!"

Avoid: "I don't need this job!"

Blame: "The problem is the people around me. I hire badly."

Counter: "There are lots of examples of me acting differently."

Attack: "I may have done this (awful thing), but you did this (other awful thing)."

Negate: "You don't really know anything about X."

Deflect: "That's not the real issue."

Invalidate: "I've asked others, and nobody agrees with the feedback."

Joke: "I never knew I was such a jerk."

Exaggerate: "This is terrible, I'm really awful."

Which of Bregman's thirteen approaches do you use to justify, rationalize, or ignore negative feedback? Most of us are so good at rejecting negative feedback that we don't even notice when we do it. It's a reflex, a knee-jerk reaction—like swatting away a mosquito buzzing around your head while you're sitting in the backyard enjoying your weekend.

You may think you're making the relationship better by pushing back against the feedback and trying to minimize it. Going back to the story about Eric's negative reaction to Morag's habitual interrupting, when Eric finally gave Morag the feedback about her interruptions, she was horrified, and then she went straight into explaining why she did it—putting a positive spin on the behavior (yep, she had forgotten our advice from earlier, to simply acknowledge the feedback with a well-timed "thank you"). The message Eric heard from Morag was "Yes, that's true about me, and it's a good thing. I just get really excited."

Eric's first thought was "I don't care how excited you are. It sucks and it contributes to the continuation of my story about you." Eric and Morag were at risk of a negative downward spiral unless they righted this relationship conversation.

As you navigate these conversations, you need to remember connection and compassion, because if someone has the guts to tell you how they're misperceiving you, you must acknowledge that, correct it, and thank them for caring enough to provide the feedback. If you don't, the conversation will freeze, and you'll remain stuck in those misperceptions.

Pro tip: it's time to stop wasting time hurting ourselves or others with made-up stories. We need to change our stories, beginning right now. To change our stories, we need to be present. We need to be in the moment. We need to pay attention to how we are showing up in all facets of our relationships. We need to go first so that we ensure that we work better together.

This isn't the time for righteous indignation: it doesn't really matter if you're right and they are wrong. When it comes to relationship repair, you can't afford to wait for others to simply wake up and see your magnificence.

In our example, Eric took a deep breath and shared what he was thinking: "I don't care how excited you are. It sucks and it contributes to the continuation of my story about you." The pattern was broken.

It takes a while to unlearn and relearn Ally Mindset behaviors. Morag's commitment was to try her best to wait for a natural break in the conversation—to count to three before filling that gap. Eric's and Ruby's explicit commitment was to help Morag unlearn and relearn these habits by either nudging her (in Eric's case, kicking Morag under the table when they were in a live meeting—yes, they were back to kindergarten, but it worked) or simply saying, "Hang on, I haven't quite finished my point."

Yes, it feels weird to do it. Yes, Morag feels a little embarrassed when caught interrupting again. However, she does it far less often. Remember, this isn't about perfection; it's about being better in the moment.

During a recent coaching engagement, we were partnered with William, a tech leader who has transformed his relationship from adversary to ally. Every interview we had with his key stakeholders started with, "Well, if you'd asked me about him four years ago, my answer would have been different."

Four years ago, William was a brilliant jerk. Today he's highly regarded and respected for his problem-solving capabilities and technical insight. Good news and a real-world example that it is indeed possible to come back from a career-damaging experience. However, the fact that everyone shared a version of the old William with their "If you'd asked me four years ago…" responses demonstrates that our past leadership behaviors can cast a long shadow. People remember the bad times, which continue to color the good that this leader is doing today. Thankfully, in William's case, this distant memory is fading and being replaced with the new story that showcases his positive impact on the team and project.

Remember Jesse's wall of shame story from chapter 6? Even though the wall of shame had been gone for more than three years, the memories persisted in the organization and those memories continued to influence employee behavior. People still hesitated to share work or to be creative because they knew (according to their story about Jesse) that they were going to be judged: Jesse was the bully. Relationship and reputation damage happens when expectations you have of others—or others have of you—fall short.

So, how do you avoid this?

Have the "how we work together" conversation explicitly—at the start of your working partnership and then regularly thereafter.

If you work with people whom you've known for years, you might figure, "We don't need to do that. We don't need to have an explicit conversation about how we should be working together." We call B.S.—you absolutely do need to have such a conversation. In fact, the longer you've known each other, the more important that conversation is because of all the assumptions that you're making and the things that you're taking for granted.

Don't let your misunderstood genius become someone else's brilliant jerk. Being a misunderstood genius isn't a badge of honor, nor is it "their problem." We remember well the leader we worked with in the past who used to tell his employees, "People have had problems with me my entire life, but I am willing to help *them* through it." Say what?!

If you aren't perceived as an ally, then you need to go first—to meet others where they are, to change your game, to help everyone be better in this game of work.

The responsibility belongs to all of us.

We need to work better together to do better work together.

So, what can we do?

We need a step-by-step process.

Coincidentally we just happen to have one . . .

The Plot Twist: Moving from Brilliant Jerk to Ally

Repairing a damaged relationship, or your reputation, starts with giving up something of value rather than asking for something of value from others. If you don't give first, then you are simply conducting a transaction. Think of the giving as a deposit into a relationship bank account, and in the case of a damaged relationship, a bank account that is currently overdrawn. You may need to make several deposits to get back into the black and into your colleague's good graces.

Whether you:

- Lost your temper in a meeting
- Replied all when you should've waited to respond
- Missed a critical deadline
- Told a joke—that wasn't funny

You need to get past the emotional shock of feedback that feels like a slap upside the head. Believe us, righteous indignation won't cut it—even if you're right. Denial keeps you stuck. Shame and embarrassment keep you from stepping into the arena and retaking the spotlight. Think about it. The last time you received feedback that didn't fit your self-image or your intent, what was your reaction? Bamboozled? Flabbergasted? A gut punch that made you feel sick?

If so, you likely reacted defensively and withdrew, denied the feedback, or lashed out. Instead of writing all those negative stories, and digging the hole you're standing in even deeper, adopt a three-step approach:

1 **Look up.** Assess the damage: What's your culpable negligence? What behavior do you need to own? What are the warning signs you missed? (Did you underplay the risk, or fail to act early?) How do you want others to feel in your presence? How do you feel in your own presence? (Shut up, trash talk!)

2 **Show up.** Apologize, own it, and share what you intend to do differently. Own the impact on your relationship and reputation. You can't change others; you can only change you. In your next meeting, do you need to show more compassion? Demonstrate a little less candor, and listen more? Engage in a little more debate and ask powerful questions before jumping into action? When you change how you show up, you change the course of your relationship and your leadership reputation.

3 **Step up.** Be consistent, be vigilant, be different. The key is to do your best and be your best.

Relationship and reputation damage happens when expectations you have of others—or others have of you—fall short.

Here are some more specific things you can do as you apply this step-by-step process to your own work and personal relationships.

Culpable Negligence: It Starts with You

Have a good, hard look in the mirror and be honest: Was this the first time this happened? The only time? Or is there a pattern of behavior and feedback that you need to pay attention to?

Why did you react in this particular way? What was happening that you found upsetting? Which of your values might have been transgressed or challenged?

What was the trigger? What caused the disconnect? What caused you to fluff the landing? Are there specific situations (or people) that push your buttons? Things happening at home that put you on a hair trigger at work? Once you determine the cause, you'll be in a position to anticipate those situations in the future and choose to respond, instead of just reacting.

Look for the nugget—the 1 percent of truth—as you reflect on the feedback. If the feedback is 90 percent fluff and 10 percent substance, tease out the substance. Get the perspective of an ally—not to discount the feedback, but to cut through the noise and find the golden nugget. There is almost always a grain of truth in feedback, but you don't necessarily have to act on it. That final step is your choice to make. Make it a deliberate choice, not an act of omission or denial.

No golden nugget? Then put the feedback on the shelf until it's gathered dust and is forgotten, or until a second data point emerges, at which point you can take it down and reexamine it.

Morag shares her story about taking ownership of her role in a relationship:

I had a colleague whose presence on the planet was enough to set me off. They had plenty of opinions to share about others' shortcomings, and what riled me up was that those same shortcomings were their own.

In one particularly tense meeting, I am ashamed to admit, I slammed my laptop shut in frustration and had to leave. Eric talked me down from my ledge and I returned to the meeting, apologized (the person was oblivious to my exit and return—the others in the room weren't), and we moved on.

Scene Change: Rewriting Stories

Apologize not only to the recipient of your less-than-stellar performance but also to innocent bystanders, those who witnessed the outburst or were impacted in the ripple effect of your behavior.

Try as you might to change someone else, you have to turn the light around and shine it on yourself. Ask, Why am I so teed off by this person? Why does this person rub me the wrong way all the time? Morag continues her story:

I had to rewrite my stories—what I was thinking about my colleague, how I valued them. Did it mean we became allies and best friends? No, we became, at best, supporters. But the work we were able to do together improved considerably. And that's the point: we need to work better together (despite our differences) to do better work together.

It reduced the stress and volatility of how I showed up in our meetings. My colleague may never have noticed (I didn't ask), but I know the innocent bystanders—the other team members—noticed the change and they were visibly less stressed. All that drama, which I created, helped no one, least of all myself.

What are the traits you despise in others? What are the traits you despise in yourself? Learning to accept these traits, to work with them and work around them, can be a humbling experience. But as Morag's story relates, doing so can make us more effective in our relationships, happier, and more approachable. The key for each of us is to know when our buttons are being pushed, when we're reacting, and when it's time to step back.

The Grand Finale

We all know that person who promises to be different, to do different, but nothing ever changes. Don't be that person! If you want others' (mis)perceptions of you to shift, you'll need to step up and demonstrate consistent and unfailing change in your attitude and approach.

What is one thing you could do to shift your relationship presence? Leadership coach Cynthia Burnham has a technique she uses called "until today." Cynthia has people she's working with stop their negative behavior and say, "Until today, I have been perceived as [insert the word or phrase of your choice]." This approach gives you back your power because tomorrow is a whole new day, a whole new you.

The first few times you try a new behavior (like Morag pausing and waiting to speak) your colleague may be thinking, "She's only doing it because I said something" or "The boss told her to do it." Then maybe, "Oh yeah. Let's see if she can do it. This will never last."

This is important: thanks to confirmation bias, people tend to recognize the behaviors that confirm their beliefs about others, as opposed to seeing the behaviors that are at odds with their beliefs. When you mess up again (as you certainly will), then that'll be proof for the prosecution that you weren't being genuine in trying to change, right?

When people are no longer paying attention, that means you've changed your reputation and you need to stick with it, even though it may be hard. This is when patience really is a virtue.

Don't just focus on your behaviors (what you're doing); build the bridges with your colleagues and create a genuine connection and relationship (how you relate, get to know who they are, and in doing so show who you are). As we shared earlier, people are more likely to give the benefit of the doubt to someone they know—someone they have a track record with. Even if your record is a little scratched, you don't need to lose hope. Focus on becoming the person others want to work with.

You only have so much bandwidth, and you only have so much time, effort, and energy to devote to this effort. So, you need to be picky. The way you interact with people at work is often task-driven, tactical. So, when you have a free minute, you'll tend to spend it with a person you like. And during the pandemic, that tendency was exacerbated because time became even more precious to everyone.

But there are weaker relationships across your work ecosystem, and you have to figure out how and when to put relationship capital in those banks. Sometimes you have to invest in someone you don't think you like. We say "don't think you like" because, a lot of times, you just don't know enough about who that person is to form an opinion.

Remember, most people don't get up in the morning and decide they're going to be an asshole at work that day. That's just not how people are wired. They want to do good stuff at work. They want to feel like they're reasonably connected to something larger than they are and go home at the end of the day to their family feeling good about the contributions they made. That's what people want to do.

So, giving your colleagues the benefit of the doubt and having those tough conversations with some sort of a structure are the best things you can do. And that's what this process of look up, show up, step up is all about. It's why we ended each chapter with prompts for you to look up and assess your own relationships, reflect on how you are showing up, and apply a few tactics for you to step up (differently). It's a structure to give you a place to start.

You have misperceptions about the people you work with, and they have misperceptions about you. Unfortunately those are the festering beginnings of a relationship in decay. Unless you proactively move that relationship into allyship, it will stay as it is or it will decline over time.

That obligation is on you. Even if you think the other person is a brilliant (or not-so-brilliant) jerk, it's on you. If you want it to be different, you're the only person who can make it different. You can't control what other people think about you, but you can show up differently.

When we give presentations about this concept of being an ally and what it means, someone in every crowd invariably raises their hand and asks, "So, how do I get more allies?"

Our answer?

Be one. It's the only way.

LOOK UP, SHOW UP, STEP UP

We've yet to meet anyone who deliberately set out to gain the reputation of a brilliant jerk. Rarely (other than in the movies) is someone sitting up all night plotting how to ruin your day. Most of us simply want to feel like we are adding value, doing a great job, that our opinion matters, and that we are included and a part of the team. We all will mess up at some point. If you're the one who's made a mess, here are some recommendations to repair your reputation and close your intent versus impact gap:

- **Work on yourself first.** Reputations and relationships are built (or destroyed) one conversation at time. The first step in repairing your relationship is to look at feedback you've received and honestly assess your impact. Try to see the situation from an outsider's perspective. What did you do or not do? What must be done to correct it? Consider working with an executive coach who can help you to see where your intent and impact are misaligned.

- **Say thank you.** Whether the feedback you receive is deserved or not, own the impact of your behavior. Accept the feedback with grace and say thank you. This is not the time to shoot the messenger. When you treat people well, especially the bearer of bad news, they are more likely to give you the benefit of the doubt in the future, along with the candid feedback you may need. Express gratitude, acknowledge what you have heard, and choose to admit mistakes and apologize.

- **Ask an ally.** If you're still not sure how you got into this pickle, then ask a few trusted allies who can provide more balanced views and perspectives, including on what you may have done to exacerbate the situation and what you need to do to fix it.

- **Be proactive.** Don't let your relationship wither on the vine. Be courageously vulnerable. If something is on your mind, if you know you are not at your best, let others know! Sharing—"I'm not myself today. I only got two hours of sleep last night because I was thinking about the presentation next week" or "I'm a little distracted right now. I have a personal issue that I am trying to resolve"—allows you to control the story that people might otherwise write without this information.

Take some time to reflect on the following questions to identify opportunities to strengthen your leadership reputation and impact:

- What is your leadership reputation? What three words would others use to describe you at your best and at your worst? How do these align with your intent?

- Who have you disappointed recently? Who might you be taking for granted? Who would welcome an invitation for coffee and more time with you?

- Whose advice and guidance could you benefit from? Which professional relationship would be nurtured by asking for their input and help?

TRUST

The Secret Sauce to
Friendships at Work

66

Trust is the duct tape that holds
a team together in times of
crisis and the WD-40 that enables things
to move effortlessly on sunny days.

MORAG BARRETT

WE'VE DUG DEEP into the Ally Mindset, exploring the five practices of our model and how to engage the model to change your relationships. But surprise! There's one more thing that must be in place for the Ally Mindset to work—the very human, alchemical catalyst that creates and maintains it over time.

And this one more thing is *trust*.

Trust is a bridge of connection we build with someone else that says, "I believe you; I can rely on you; I feel safe with you."

But the trust we feel with someone is in a constant state of flux, strengthened or weakened—one conversation at a time, one action at a time, one promise at a time—as we make deposits into or take withdrawals from our relationship bank account. Each interaction we have with others can either build trust or destroy it—sometimes a teeny-tiny bit and sometimes a lot, in small moments as well as the big actions in our day-to-day interactions on or off the job.

That's all well and good, but why should you bother with the trust thing? Isn't it just a fad that's going to come and go before you move on to the next management technique du jour? The answer is an emphatic *no*. In its *24th Annual Global CEO Survey*, PwC reported that in 2020, a lack of trust was one of the top twenty threats that CEOs saw to their organizations' growth prospects. Trust is clearly a game changer and something we need a lot more of in our organizations, not less.

As Morag points out in the quote that opens this chapter, trust has two key elements:

- It's sticky, holding relationships together when times get tough—when the proverbial shit hits the fan

- It's slippery, easing relationships into a warm and comfortable safe space that allows us to work easily together without having to waste energy making furtive glances over our shoulders, anxious that someone might be sneaking up to stab us in the back

The Ally Mindset enables you to move from the *me-first* to the *we-first* perspective that maximizes your potential to be and have allies. These two elements of trust work together in balance, providing the tasty secret sauce you need to be an ally to those around you.

But there's one more level of trust that many often forget. In addition to trust (or a lack thereof) in others, there is trust (or a lack thereof) in yourself. And like the trust you have with others, this, too, is in a constant state of flux, a constant state of change. If you've ever heard that insidious little voice in your head telling you, "You're not ready," "You messed up," "You can't [insert your dream]," even when others are telling you that you're great, then you'll understand what we mean. Why is it that we can *give* trust to others, and yet sometimes distrust and doubt ourselves, even in the face of the overwhelming trust and confidence we regularly receive *from* others?

The Ally Mindset isn't only about how you show up with others: it's how you show up and believe in and trust yourself.

Do you articulate your needs and ask for what you want, or do you hope others will read your mind and figure out your needs for themselves? (Good luck with that!) And when they don't read your mind and respond in kind, you might lose a bit of trust with yourself as you beat yourself up for your lack of candor. Do you give yourself the benefit of the doubt? The grace and space to take informed risk in pursuit of your goals?

As you consider your own relationships with others, ask yourself these questions: When do I give trust explicitly and implicitly? When do I withhold it? How do I earn trust, become trustworthy? And how does trust get broken?

Keep in mind that people don't solely base trust on the personal, one-on-one interactions you have with them. They're also observing your interactions with others—big and small, each and every day, and over long periods of time—and their trust in you (or a lack thereof) reflects that.

Do you treat others with respect, or do you consider them to be akin to the reeking bag of garbage you threw in the trash can last night? Do you really listen to what they say, or do you ignore their good ideas—thinking your own are the only ideas worth considering? Do you follow through on your commitments to others, or do you quickly forget you even made them?

People are watching you, and they're calibrating their trust in you based on what they see and hear from others—good and bad.

Trust is an enigma wrapped in a riddle. We know when it's missing, but we're often oblivious to trust when it is present. It's nebulous, touchy-feely to the extreme, and yet fundamental to everything we do in life. Our ability to take (informed) risks, look outward, celebrate others through abundance and generosity, connect with compassion, demonstrate courage and vulnerability, express candor and debate, and take action and accountability all depend on trust.

**Relationships are built
or destroyed one conversation
at a time, one action
(or lack of action) at a time.**

When Trust Erodes

Ruby saw her friend's name flash up on her smartphone's display, and she knew immediately what the message would be: she couldn't make it to lunch after all and would need to reschedule. On the one hand, the bonus couple of hours released back into Ruby's schedule were going to be very useful; she had some serious deadlines approaching on projects that could use some extra care and attention. On the other hand, Ruby rolled her eyes as her friend once again lived up to her reputation of being a no-show.

Ruby enjoyed her friend's company when they did get together, and her friend often suggested that the two should collaborate on client projects together. But guess what? That collaboration was never going to happen. Why not? Because a vital connection was missing in their relationship: trust. How could Ruby trust her friend with the big commitments involved in executing a client project—putting SkyeTeam's and her own good reputation on the line—if she couldn't trust her with a little commitment like getting together for lunch?

Over a period of years, the trust Ruby had originally felt with her friend had been slowly eroded as each commitment was postponed, pushed aside, or canceled altogether.

Now before you start with "Yes, but..." some of the friend's reasons for bailing at the last minute were entirely valid. However, it was the ongoing pattern of behavior that had become an issue.

Here's another example of how trust erodes over time. Morag's son was bemoaning the team he had been assigned for a college class project. As often happens, some members of the team were sitting back and contributing absolutely nothing. Maybe they were working off the ill effects of a hangover or dreaming about where they would go for spring break, but that was about it.

Since his grade, and the grade of everyone else on the team, hinged on this project's outcome, he was frustrated, and rightly so. He couldn't trust the slackers to step up and do their part; the evidence so far indicated that they were completely unreliable. So, Morag's son banded together with his engaged classmates to step up and invest the extra time required to fill the gap, for their own good. The slackers, of course, also benefited without lifting a finger. Until, that is, the professor asked about the collective work effort of the team.

Without the team needing to say anything, the professor shared his perspective on who he believed had ensured team success. And he was right. The slackers shifted uncomfortably in their seats. They apologized to the rest of the team and took an adjustment to their project grade that the professor applied. The message was delivered and received, and there was more engagement on the next group project.

That situation demonstrates not just a personal challenge but a professional malaise. This soap opera plays out time and time again at work, school, community-based organizations, churches, sports teams, and anywhere else you don't get to choose your colleagues. The stakes are high at an individual team and organizational level, where reputations are at risk and business results are jeopardized when you don't trust your colleagues.

If you're a leader in your organization (whatever your level or career stage), we guarantee that someone is always watching you. Question is, are others watching and admiring you, wanting to work with and for you? Or are they grateful you aren't part of their immediate team? You get to choose.

Whether you are in a corporate role, a solopreneur, part of a family unit, or in any other relationship, you are dependent on others to achieve your goals, whether it's as simple as getting groceries into the refrigerator, a bit more complicated like gathering the information required to achieve the next project milestone, or extremely complex like orchestrating a multistage sequence of events over months that leads to a major accomplishment and organizational transformation.

And the years we operated in "pandemic mode" put a serious dent in our ability to nurture relationships, to make deposits into the trust bank accounts. We've spent much of this time cut off from our normal routines and isolated from colleagues, friends, and family. We've been cut off from the proverbial watercooler and the opportunities it provides for socializing at the office. And many of us, leaders included, are still struggling to find our way with remote or hybrid work.

Has your success been undermined by the words or actions of a colleague? If you are in a corporate role, then the answer is likely to be yes, and it sucks. Stress levels invariably go up, and relationship health deteriorates. In our experience, most people don't wake up in the morning with the intent of undermining others (of course, there are always going to be a few exceptions—there are toxic people and bad bosses in most any organization). However, intention and impact are occasionally misaligned.

We've said it before, and we'll say it again: work is the biggest team sport any of us get to participate in. We are all dependent on others to achieve our goals—especially as our goals scale in size and complexity.

So, why the disconnect?

How You Know Trust Is Lacking

How do you know when you don't have trust in a relationship?

When you can't feel its presence.

Your intuition or instincts scream out to you, "Danger, Will Robinson!" like the robot on *Lost in Space*. (Not that we're old enough to have watched that iconic 1960s TV show ourselves!) If you've ever worked with someone you don't trust (and, as our research shows, that's 67 percent of you), what was the soundtrack playing in your head? And where exactly did you feel that distrust physically? Did you feel a knot in your stomach? A sense of dread and foreboding tingling its way down your spine? An uptick in your anxiety level?

Which working relationships do you think are the most troublesome? Which are the most difficult for you? According to our research, the most problematic relationships are with:

- Peers elsewhere in the org (28.5 percent)
- Colleagues in senior positions (19.8 percent)
- Peers within the same team/function (11.4 percent)
- External customers (5.5 percent)
- Direct reports (3.0 percent)

So, as you can see, the biggest problem most of us have is with people at the same level as us, outside our own team or department. That is followed by people who are higher up in the organization.

And here are some of the many ways that people's trust was broken by someone they worked with:

- "Team leader taking credit for my suggestion, my process maps, guides, support, and training documents. She got a bonus, and I didn't."

- "My manager wants to be liked by everyone but is fake. He is also a micromanager that doesn't think anyone can do the job but himself. He regularly undermines everything we do. My direct coworker sees me as competition, so he undercuts my fees."

- "I was managing a project that my peer did not want to be a part of but was required to be. She constantly pushed back and delayed progress, which caused friction for the entire team."

- "I had a coworker who purposely kept important project details to himself, as well as mistakes he'd made, but presented it as my fault to executives to save his own job. Unfortunately they believed him without talking to me first."

- "Someone senior to me did not invite me to a social function which seemed to be open to everyone else."

We could go on and on with these personal anecdotes submitted by people who took our survey—we have hundreds of them. Of course, there are all sorts of ways that trust breaks down in an organization. Here's just a small handful of commonly encountered behaviors that indicate a lack of trust. Note that each of these bullet points contains a pair of behaviors that are opposites:

- Arriving late for meetings *or* arriving early for meetings (trust us—we've heard complaints for both)

- Not doing the required research or prework for a meeting *or* overpreparing

- Faking it until they (don't) make it, leaving others to fill in the gaps to avoid dropping the ball *or* running away with the ball and not letting others play

- Badmouthing or talking about colleagues, customers, vendors, or anyone else behind their backs *or* sweet-talking and not sharing the truth

- Double-checking work and constantly checking up on people *or* letting standards drop because you've lost faith and
  no longer care what happens next

- BMWing (yes, that still stands for bitching, moaning, and
  whining) at the end of the day to anyone who will listen *or*
  putting on a brave face and not speaking your truth

Since each of the opposite behaviors above indicates a lack
of trust, how are you supposed to know when trust is lacking?
That's exactly our point.

As leaders, when you don't trust the people who work for
and with you, you tend to micromanage them—checking up
on them more frequently rather than checking in with them.
As a result, the answer to the questions "Can I count on you?"
and "Can I depend on you?" becomes a self-fulfilling no.
When managers decide to do the work themselves instead
of delegating it to their people, they naturally become aloof
and dispassionate. When asked the question "Do I care about
you?" their actions say no.

While the intent of all your micromanaging may be to
avoid failure or mistakes, constantly looking over others'
shoulders (and second-guessing or anticipating their decisions)
is a recipe for frustration, demotivation, and disengagement.
And not just for the hapless employees who work for you, but
for you, too, as you rail against having to "do it all myself." It's
important to note that the behaviors that demonstrate trust
or a lack of trust aren't always mirror images of each other.

A group of professors in the US and China conducted a
series of field studies to get to the heart of the specific behaviors that shape people's perception of leaders' competence,
trustworthiness, and credibility. According to their findings,

published in the MIT *Sloan Management Review*, leaders are viewed as untrustworthy when they:

- Promote an unethical climate in the organization
- Communicate dishonestly
- Act in a self-serving manner
- Behave in an inconsistent manner
- Communicate in a guarded or inconsistent manner
- Ignore the input of employees and key stakeholders
- Treat employees as expendable

In addition, the studies found that leaders are viewed as incompetent when they:

- Fail to demonstrate relevant knowledge and expertise
- Fail to take appropriate actions
- Take ego-driven actions
- Fail to appreciate employees
- Create confusion among employees and key stakeholders
- Communicate poorly
- Are closed-minded

When leaders are considered to be both untrustworthy and incompetent by those around them, they're totally screwed. Their credibility is shot, and they'll be lucky to get anyone to follow their lead. According to the researchers, "It's more difficult to regain credibility once it's lost than to build credibility in the first place." But, as the researchers also pointed out, leaders can restore their lost credibility by repeatedly engaging in trustworthy acts and by "emphasizing the specific behaviors that project competence and trustworthiness."

When leaders are viewed as trustworthy, according to this research, they:

- Communicate and act in a consistent manner
- Protect the organization and employees
- Embody the organization's vision and values
- Consult with and listen to key stakeholders
- Communicate openly with others
- Value employees
- Offer support to employees and key stakeholders

And as the research revealed, leaders are seen as competent when they:

- Emphasize the future
- Emphasize organizational outcomes
- Emphasize employees
- Take action and initiative
- Communicate effectively
- Gain knowledge and experiences

Some of the findings of this research are particularly interesting to us because, on the surface, they don't seem to go together. For example, leaders who emphasize the future are seen as competent. That's the highest correlated trait there. The second highest correlated trait is emphasizing organizational outcomes and the third is emphasizing people.

So, if a leader is focused on the future, focused on what the organization is trying to accomplish, and focused on their people, then they're perceived as highly competent. However, not even one of those qualities directly correlates to their personal competence. These are all relationship-oriented factors.

And the same goes with the trustworthiness side of the research. If the leader is consistent in their communications

The Ally Mindset
begins with *you*.

and actions, if they seem protective of the organization and their people, and if they embody the vision and values of the organization, they are perceived as more trustworthy. Again these are relationship-oriented factors.

The point is, you can up how competent and trustworthy people perceive you as by dialing into your relationships with the people who work for and with you. It's those relationship-oriented elements that are the key drivers in competence and trustworthiness. And that's what we're talking about here—being the oil that keeps the relationships going as well as engagement and productivity up.

Where Do You Place Your Trust?

Which brings us to a crucial question: where do you place your trust—and where do you withhold it—in your day-to-day relationships and encounters with coworkers, customers, vendors, and others in your work and personal life? If you take a close look at this, you might be surprised at what you find out.

Let's take a moment to reflect on where you put your trust. Sit back and relax. Don't worry—your email and text messages will be there when you return in a few minutes. Promise.

Think back to the last time you took a flight somewhere. Perhaps it was a business trip or a much-delayed vacation with a significant other. Recall the excitement you felt (warning: author hyperbole incoming) arriving at the airport with plenty of time to spare (where did all the traffic go?), the warm welcome from the TSA crew as you passed through the surprisingly short security line, then making your way to the gate and eventually boarding and being ushered to your seat in a relaxed, orderly manner. There was even plenty of room in the overhead bins for your bulky carry-on, and the obligatory squalling baby was twenty-five rows behind you—well out of the auditory pain zone. Okay, maybe we're being a little bit unrealistic here, but bear with us.

As you settled into your seat, did you give a thought to the pilot and crew? Did you question whether they were going to get you to your chosen destination, on time and in one piece? We're going to guess that you probably did not.

If this is indeed the case, then what you did was give implicit trust to this group of people who quite literally had your life and well-being in their hands. You assumed they had been well trained, had plenty of experience, and they hadn't spent a couple of hours at the hotel bar nursing a double Scotch on the rocks before they boarded your flight.

So, if you are so quick to trust people you have never met and do not personally know, why would you withhold trust from your colleagues? The individuals with whom you closely work, day in and day out. The people whose help and support you need to get things done and accomplish your goals and the goals of your organization.

Why is it that we can give trust to a stranger or to others to take the lead on a project but then doubt ourselves? If we don't believe in ourselves, if we aren't allies to ourselves, how can we hope and expect others to be allies to us?

Chances are, they won't be.

Keep in mind that we aren't talking about giving blind or misplaced trust, such as assigning someone to be the project lead when they have a track record of dropping the ball and failing to perform. That's simply poor management. You should never assign responsibilities to someone who has proven they can't handle them. And you shouldn't take on a project yourself if you have no relevant experience and no expectation of gaining the necessary experience in time to do the assignment right and within the required schedule.

This is about giving and accepting trust—within guardrails.

If I'm new to your team, take some time to sit down with me and show some interest in my backstory, my experiences, and my life outside work. What makes me thrive? What am I passionate about? What are my hot buttons? What does success look like for me? And then reciprocate—share with me your expectations, your style, and how you want to connect. Let me know that as my boss, you may have to give tough feedback in the future. Ask me how I prefer to receive those messages so I'm receptive to them, instead of defensive about them.

This may appear to be common sense, a simple task, but it always amazes us how few leaders actually sit down with a new employee to align expectations. Not just on what tasks that new employee is expected to do, but how they will work together, who they are as people, and how they will relate.

While some people withhold trust until a person proves they are trustworthy, others give trust blindly, only to withdraw it when that trust is violated. We're always somewhat surprised when we feel that our trust in someone has been misplaced. But when we reflect on it, it isn't always because they were wrong. Sure, sometimes it is. But mostly it's because we never said, "You know what? I trust you. I believe in you. And here's what success looks like. Oh, and please don't do these particular things because it's going to push my buttons and destroy trust."

Sangita was highly regarded for her technical expertise, but her peers described her as aloof and sensed that Sangita preferred to keep her professional relationships at arm's length. It wasn't that she was leaning out of the team or didn't participate in team meetings. Sangita spoke up, and others listened. However, it didn't feel like she was leaning in to her team either; there was an invisible barrier around her. That is, until that barrier started to dissolve.

Ruby was leading Sangita's team through a discussion of the Relationship Ecosystem and applying the concepts to the team dynamic. The team enthusiastically explored the Ally Mindset practices, focusing on which of the behaviors they were demonstrating consistently and where they needed to give more care and attention. The team quickly moved to self-congratulations, believing they had one another's backs, that they were allies, and that this group was close to performing at its very best.

Sangita listened as a few members of the team announced that this was one of the best teams they had ever been on. They affirmed the need for trust and believed they had it; however, they were quick to gloss over the emotional ties that make for a true ally relationship. It was then that Sangita shared her own experience.

"This isn't a high trust team," Sangita interjected. "I'm not sure we are all allies, and until today, I didn't feel it was a safe place to share my thoughts."

There was an audible gasp from some team members. But Sangita wasn't done yet. She continued:

When I first joined this team, I was so excited to be here, until I wasn't. You may not remember, but the tipping point was an early team meeting where we were discussing a customer challenge my team was experiencing. Believing you were my allies—though we didn't have that language then—I offered my thoughts on how we could resolve it and shared some of the skill gaps I'd observed with my new team.

Two things happened that destroyed my trust in this team. First, my suggestion for how we could resolve the customer challenge wasn't just thrown out, it was clobbered. I felt personally attacked. Second, I was shocked and disappointed when the conversation about individual members of my team was repeated back to me the next week by a third party. I thought our conversation was private, that it would be held in confidence.

That destroyed my trust in this team. Since then, I've hesitated to share my true thoughts. It didn't feel like a safe space any longer. I stopped opening up, sharing the problems I saw, or asking for your input. I've not had the courage to be vulnerable again . . . until today.

Fortunately the conversations I've had in this session with some of you and the exercises Ruby has facilitated with us have started to rebuild my trust in this team. I still feel cautious, but I also feel cautiously optimistic that we can become a high trust team again—together.

In that moment, Sangita displayed several practices of the Ally Mindset: the courage and vulnerability to share what she was truly feeling, the candor and debate that helped the team to reflect on her experience, and together the action and accountability to ensure things were different in the future. Sangita wasn't asking the team to solve the breakdown in trust right then and there; she instead shone a spotlight on her lived experience and asked the team to acknowledge it.

It was the catalyst for change, and stories were rewritten: Sangita wasn't aloof; she was protecting herself from the risk of more broken confidences and trust. Sangita and the team let out a collective sigh of relief. The elephant in the room had been named, its influence already diminished, and the work to become a team of allies could begin. All because Sangita chose to go first.

Relationships are built or destroyed one conversation at a time, and if you skip the conversation about the Four Yeses and what it means to be an ally on your team, then you shouldn't be surprised if relationship ties remain weak. Trust relies on being able to say yes to these four questions:

1   Can I count on you?
2   Can I depend on you?
3   Do I care about you?
4   Do I trust you?

Our goal in an ally relationship is to be able to say yes to each of these questions, and conversely that the other person can ultimately say yes about us:

1   Can you count on me?
2   Can you depend on me?
3   Do I show that I care about you?
4   Do I make you feel safe to trust me?

The Ally Mindset isn't
only about how you show up
with others: it's how
you show up and believe in
and trust yourself.

Back in the old days when we were all bumping around the same office space for hours on end, these questions were a lot easier to answer. Can you count on me? Sure. I show up every day; you can see me at my desk working away diligently. Can you depend on me? Absolutely. I'm the one who will tell you that you've still got a little lettuce in your teeth after we come back from lunch. I give you that knowing nod in the meeting when you step up to the podium. My Spidey sense tingles when you feel a little off, and I ask if you're okay.

Those more transactional questions (Can you count on me? Can you depend on me?) are pretty easy to answer when we have context. Relationships in two dimensions rob us of almost all this context. We now go from Zoom meeting to Teams call to Meet gathering. Our happy hours and social events have looked a whole lot like work, and we just don't have the volume of serendipitous conversations that used to provide us with so much rich context.

The transformational questions about care and trust are even harder to address in today's increasingly complex world. It's a lot more complicated for me to show you that I care about you. I have to crank that dial *way* up to even move the needle. I have to do something like write a thank-you note on a paper card with some sort of ink stick, put a government sticker (that keeps going up in price) on it, and put it in a box where someone else magically makes it show up at your house (at arm's length). And building trust is a complex beast when all the dominos are lined up perfectly. In this disjointed space, we must go first, be authentic, and work that one conversation at a time.

As we discussed earlier, building trust in an organization depends on employees feeling psychologically safe. This means being able to ask "dumb" questions, to step outside the status quo, and to make mistakes without being punished for them. Psychological safety is widely believed to be the foundation for every high-performing team and organization. At the very heart of high-performing teams and organizations are trusting professional relationships.

Can I Count On You?

The ability to count on someone is table stakes for any relationship. It's the DWYSYWD—do what you say you will do. It's purely transactional. The challenge comes if we haven't clarified expectations and definitions of success: "I want a box" versus "I want a twelve-inch square box with a sparkly purple bow." Don't be surprised if you get an envelope instead of a box, and certainly don't begrudge the colleague who brought it to you.

The stakes get higher when you have to rely on a colleague who has a spotty track record. When Morag's son gets the same flaky students assigned to his next team, he will likely expect that they will let him down. Of course, that doesn't have to be the case at all—for Morag's son or for anyone who is stuck in a similar situation.

You can break the cycle by starting the next project with a candid conversation that resets expectations. Provide feedback based on past experiences where expectations were missed and where their work wasn't at the expected standard. We often ask leaders we are coaching if they have provided feedback to the person who has missed their expectations, and if the other person knows their frustrations. The answer we get is usually a resounding no. Well, none of us are mind readers (spoiler alert), and we can't fix a problem that we don't know exists.

If you want to count on me, I must know your expectations.

If you want me to count on you, I need to know what to expect.

Pop star Bruno Mars had it right when he sang about the importance of having friends you can count on in his aptly titled song "Count On Me." It comes down to the dialogue: sharing expectations (our individual understanding) and identifying where we are in alignment, where we disagree, and where we lack clarity. Here are some things you can do to break the cycle of missed expectations:

- Follow up and document how you are going to move forward together.

- If one of you forgets or missteps, give the benefit of the doubt and provide the feedback or ask a question immediately. Don't wait for another infraction as you are likely to jump to the "case for the prosecution" versus the "advocate for the defense" when you do.

- Ask for feedback during and at the end of projects: what worked and what didn't, and how the team worked together. Make this a two-way dialogue instead of a one-way monologue.

- Share the potential consequences or impact of missed expectations. For example, "I need that by Thursday so we can send everything to the printer and get it to the participants in time for their program."

- Include others as appropriate before issues arise. That way you aren't risking the misperception that you've thrown someone under the bus.

- End meetings with clear next steps and send a short email detailing who is doing what by when. If someone drops the ball, you can seek guidance from others. For example, "Sarah hasn't sent me the final design files, which means we can't send everything to the printers as we agreed. What do you suggest I do next?"

Can I Depend On You?

Rachel is the owner of a small leadership training firm and a good friend of SkyeTeam, one of our extended posse whom we trust to cofacilitate our programs. Depending on the needs of both our firms, we can either be working closely together for a few months or spending a little time on our own projects. Ruby remembers thinking, "I haven't heard from Rachel in a while. I wonder what's happening in her world."

Ruby called Rachel, and when Rachel picked up the phone, she was crying. At that very moment, she was home alone bawling. She felt completely overwhelmed about things in her business. It turned out that Rachel had just hung up from a call with a client who was asking for more work (hurrah!) than she could possibly deliver in the time frame requested (oh no!)—especially with her already heavy workload (yikes!). She was feeling stressed and vulnerable, and being a solopreneur, she believed she had no one to turn to and that she had to navigate this moment alone.

That's the heart of the question "Can I depend on you?" It's not only about the contracted moments—can you facilitate this workshop on this date?—where SkyeTeam is depending on Rachel. It's reciprocal, with Rachel knowing that she can depend on us, something we'd obviously failed to communicate! It's thinking, "I have some space in my schedule. I wonder what's going on with this person. Do they need anything this week that I can provide? How can I support them?" It's a way to build trust and connection.

So, there Rachel was, in tears, running out of time, and feeling completely alone. If one of us hadn't checked in with her that day, we would have never known. She may have had several more days of deep distress in isolation. This lack of awareness of others' situations has only increased in the hybrid working environment. Who do you need to check on today?

"Can I count on you?" is reactive, whereas "Can I depend on you?" (and "Can others depend on you?") is proactive. It's the discretionary effort, a willingness to take informed risk (candor and debate) or step into the arena and assume additional responsibilities (action and accountability).

When you can depend on someone, and they can depend on you, you're going beyond the immediate task at hand, which means you need to understand what else is on your colleague's plate. It's unfair to expect to depend on someone who is being pulled in multiple directions and has competing priorities. When you only focus on your priorities and don't clarify where they fall on someone else's to-do list, how can you expect to get the turnarounds, support, care, and attention you need? It may be at the top of your list today, and number fifteen on your colleague's. An Ally Mindset pauses to ask, clarify, and align expectations on all sides.

Another person's ability to depend on you is an element that comes with time, and if past performance has left the relationship wanting, then you need to change how you show up. You can't change someone else, but you can change how you are perceived. Again, clarify what you expect and what you will or won't do in the relationship (for example, "I can't work weekends but can work late on Thursdays"). Talk about how you will raise the flag, or expect them to, before issues become barriers to mutual success.

It's easier to trust when stakes are low, when there is only one right answer, when everyone agrees. The true test is in those high stakes moments—the system outage, the irate major client, the resignation of your star player, a global pandemic—and then you find out who you can trust in an emergency.

In *Cultivate*, Morag talks about the importance of prioritizing your stakeholder relationships, of investing extra care and attention in those critical few. If you've invested in your relationships, then you know who you can depend on, and they know that they can depend on you.

If you're working with someone who has let you down in the past, or with whom you have tense interactions, now is the time to reset expectations to make sure they don't continue to take advantage. It's horrid working with colleagues you don't trust, and it drains energy to continually worry about being let down or getting a knife in the back. Don't ignore your Spidey sense. Speak up and ask for what you want and need. If you own how you show up, you can influence the outcome. And you never know, you might just transform a distrustful relationship into one that is Four Yeses.

Do I Care about You?

It's hard to care about someone you know nothing about. You've been blindsided by the words or actions of a colleague, held your tongue instead of speaking up, or softened a message for fear of others' reactions: each of these situations indicates a lack of connection. A lack of connection can be a hard gap to bridge during the best of times; however, the COVID-19 pandemic only widened that gap.

Microsoft reviewed collaboration trends in billions of Microsoft Teams and Outlook interactions during the period of February 2020 through January 2021. The results of their research show that interactions within immediate teams (close networks) strengthened with the move to remote work, and that interactions outside immediate teams (distant networks) diminished.

That may not sound like a big deal, but the fact is we are becoming more siloed, which is not a good thing for any organization. Silos create walls between people, breaking their connections. As Microsoft senior principal researcher Dr. Nancy Baym explains, "When you lose connections, you stop innovating. It's harder for new ideas to get in and groupthink becomes a serious possibility."

Microsoft's findings are reinforced in the feedback we are hearing from the leaders with whom we work. Even within intact teams that meet regularly, the sense of connection is declining. And when we look at the horizontal relationships upstream and downstream and between teams, we can see that the ties are weaker, and the relationships are deteriorating further. You can see in Microsoft's graph in their report that the lines crossed just as COVID took hold in March 2020 and companies sent their employees home en masse.

As connections erode and relationships deteriorate, so does trust. The result is slower information sharing, increased information hoarding (after all, knowledge is power, right?), a breakdown in creativity and innovation, and much more. We are less able to respond at speed and with agility. And as evidenced by the Great Resignation, we are also potentially risking major disengagement and turnover, and in many cases experiencing it for ourselves.

The pandemic caused many employees to feel increased burnout, grief, and exhaustion. Employees also report wanting to feel valued and treated as individuals (which is made more challenging in a hybrid environment). According to McKinsey research, not feeling valued by one's manager

(52 percent) and not feeling a sense of belonging (51 percent) were two commonly cited reasons why people said they left a job during a six-month period ending in November 2021.

During that same six-month period, McKinsey's study also found that one of the top five reasons why employees decided to stay at a job was because they worked with people who trust and care for one another (48 percent): "Level of trust in and care for teammates contributes to the perception of psychological safety—reinforcing or weakening adaptability. The greater the psychological safety, the more quickly belonging, engagement, and ability to deal with stress can improve because people feel supported."

And yet organizations and leaders are relying on transactional strategies (the first two questions) to try to keep their team members. As this data shows, if you want to stem the tide of the Great Resignation, you must address the relationship factor and our need for connection and well-being. And even absent the Great Resignation, a toxic relationship with a boss or colleagues and not feeling a sense of belonging are consistently in the top reasons cited for leaving an organization (along with leaving for higher pay, career advancement, and so on). The Great Resignation is simply amplifying and accelerating those exit decisions.

As leaders, we are team members and human beings too (yes, really!). Developing your Ally Mindset isn't solely about paying attention and meeting the needs of your team and employees. It's also making the time for and prioritizing your own needs. Making the effort to strengthen the relational ties you have with your colleagues is, and always was, the secret to high performance and talent retention.

Millions of employees onboarded during the pandemic, and this sense of disconnection is understandable. Right now there's a squeeze on talent, and a lot of people are in

Trust is strengthened in the spaces between the work.

new jobs and have yet to meet the people they work with in person. They don't have the spontaneous hallway and water-cooler conversations; they don't get to walk to meetings and go to lunch together and do all the other everyday things that naturally allow us to build connection and trust with our colleagues.

If we are assigned to a project together and we've never met before, trust may be reserved and one or both of us may be a little nervous about how this project is going to unfold. Even if we have worked together for decades, I might be carrying baggage about the success (or failure) of our last collaboration, and this may undermine the level of trust in our relationship. But here's the kicker: if I've never mentioned what's bugging me, you may not be aware there is an issue!

What Can We Do to Build Trust?

Remember, relationships are built or destroyed one conversation at a time, one action (or lack of action) at a time. Trust is both art and science in action. It may have a foundation in logic and the transaction (DWYSYWD), but it is amplified and reinforced through emotion—how you feel about each other. You can turn the tide toward building relationships and trust by nurturing an employees' sense of connection and belonging before you focus on the work to be done. The friendship factor becomes the *we-first* multiplier. For example, check in with an employee to see *how* they are doing, not just *what* they are doing.

Here are some tips for building connection and trust:

Set up time to talk through expectations for a project and how you will work together. Explain where roles and responsibilities stop and start, or where they overlap, and how you'll hold each other accountable. Are you going to pause peri-odically to make sure everything's on track and do regular retrospectives? If you've worked together before, use this as an opportunity to recalibrate and reset expectations.

Ask questions, channel your curiosity, and explore ways forward together to uncover potential hurdles. Explore the possible challenges you'll face before you run into them and make plans for dealing with them when they invariably happen. As every manager knows all too well, people are messy. It's what happens when people work together. You're going to step on one another's toes. You're going to bump into each other. You're occasionally going to hurt someone's feelings, even when you don't mean to. If you acknowledge up front that that's going to happen and have a plan for how you're going to deal with it, you'll be better off. And you'll be much more keyed in to assuming positive intent and trusting one another.

Agree on milestones and how you will check in on each other. When you do this in advance, it's much less likely that you checking in will be misinterpreted as lack of trust or micro-management. Ask and discuss "How are we going to measure our success? What are we going to do if we're not success-ful?" Make a habit of checking in with your people, instead of checking up on them. There's a big difference.

We're a little bit vulnerable here at SkyeTeam; when we check in, we let our guard down, and we openly share our client hits and misses. Sometimes there's laughter and some-times there are tears. When we talk about a client-facing issue that didn't go as well as we hoped it would, we focus on figur-ing out how to do better next time. When we share a success, it's usually immediately followed by a heartfelt expression of gratitude to someone on the team who made that success pos-sible. It's completely changed the tenor of our staff meetings.

Schedule spontaneity and a little fun into your working relationships. Bring your human to work (you've got one, right?), and you may just surprise each other. The key to this is making sure that you actually do it.

Keep in mind that different people have different ideas of what constitutes fun at work; it depends on preferences and tendencies, and how they are wired. There are some people who don't think you should have fun at work. Let's be clear, those people are wrong. When you're spontaneous and inject some fun into the workplace, you lower the barriers that separate us, and you enable people to become more authentically human. Doing so is your best shot at deepening trust across all your working relationships.

So What? Now What?

As we put the wraps on this final chapter, we would like to point out something that we consider to be absolutely critical to establishing and growing trust between you and others—at work and in your personal life. Throughout this book, we've made the point loud and clear that the Ally Mindset begins with *you*. If you wait for others to reach out to you to be your ally, you might be waiting a very long time. Instead of waiting for others to reach out to you, reach out to them first. Act today, right this very minute. Don't put it off another moment.

Similarly, building trust requires you to take the first step. And this begins with looking at where your relationships with each of your critical stakeholders stands.

Trust isn't something to keep within you, bottled up and doled out only on rare occasions. Trust is something you should give freely to others: the people you work and live with, and even people you've just met. When you do, you set yourself up for connection—and you build the Ally Mindset.

Trust is the true currency in any organization, the coinage that impacts your reputation and influence as a leader. We challenge you not to wait to be paid in trust, but to define for yourself what it means to give trust, to be trustworthy, to be trusted. Do this by exploring what you look to in others and what others need from you, and then choose to go first, to give first, to show up as an ally. How do you want others to feel in your presence? Trusted and trusting.

Relationships come and go throughout our lives and careers. The context for the relationship changes; goals and priorities shift; colleagues are promoted and transferred; reporting assignments are changed. However, your success is dependent on others, and their success is dependent on you. There will be people who can help, and people who have a damaged relationship with you or one that has not yet started.

What is your relationship reputation and impact? Today is the day to effect change, to repair damaged relationships, and to leverage the power of your winning relationships.

Be intentional in how you show up. Articulate your wants, needs, and expectations. Ensure alignments and intentionally nurture and build relationships with every coworker.

All we can ask of you is to do your best. Remember the immortal words of Yoda: "Do. Or do not. There is no try."

Now, get out there and *do*.

LOOK UP, SHOW UP, STEP UP

Trust is both art and science based in the logic and transaction of behaviors and results, and trust is strengthened and reinforced in the spaces between the work—in the relationship, feelings, and sense of connection we create between us. To improve how you build trust:

- **Make time alone to improve time together.** It may sound like an oxymoron, but spending time alone with your own thoughts, reading, or walking—however you want to experience the alone time (bubble bath, anyone?)—gives you an opportunity for distance and perspective. When you disengage from the daily hubbub and hustle, your mind will often provide insight into the quality of your relationships. You can then reengage more powerfully when you return to your work team and family dynamics.

- **Give your full attention.** How many times has someone asked you if you have a minute, and while the answer was no, you let them chat anyway—but your mind was focused on what you could or should be doing? If you want to increase trust, pay attention, as every conversation matters. Give people the courtesy of your time, put everything aside, and give them your full attention. Don't interrupt (Morag, listen up!); let them finish their request. If what they really need requires more than a minute, say, "This sounds important. Let's schedule time [today, tomorrow, etc.] so I can give you the attention it deserves."

- **Align expectations.** One of the most powerful things you can do to build trust is to align expectations and discuss what a high trust relationship means for each of you and how you will work together, not just what results need to be delivered.

Ensure the implicit is explicit and the rules of engagement are clear. It is then easier to build from this foundation of trust and to course correct as needed, especially in times of stress and uncertainty when trust can be challenged.

- **Make connection a habit.** Trust comes from being authentic, both to yourself and when sharing your story. Relationships become more vibrant when you feel a sense of connection, whether that's over a mutual love of cats, salsa dancing, or a laser-like ability to get to the underlying issue when solving work problems.

- **Routinely practice gratitude and thanks by sending some love.** Who needs to hear a positive message? Call them and leave a voicemail to thank them for their contribution. Contact employees, colleagues, customers, vendors, and so on to let them know you are thinking of them without asking for or needing something in return.

As you consider the trust profile for each of your critical stakeholders, take some time to reflect on the following questions:

- Are you a give first or wait first when it comes to trust? How has this served you in the past?

- In which relationships do you need to give trust? Repair trust? Earn trust? What are your first steps to increase the level of trust in these relationships?

- In what way do you need to show up differently to demonstrate your Ally Mindset and approach to collaboration? How might this change the stories and ultimately the results you create together?

- Where does the needle on your trust barometer point in key relationships? High? Fair? Low? What could you give to increase your trust in others and thereby increase their trust in you?

- What might you need to apologize for?

- What do you need to ask for going forward to better articulate and meet your needs?

ALWAYS DO YOUR BEST

66

Under any circumstance,
always do your best,
no more and no less.

DON MIGUEL RUIZ

WE KNOW THAT the advice we have given to you in this book is easier said than done. The ideas are simple—we're not talking rocket science here—but implementing these ideas and turning them into everyday habits can be a tremendous challenge. We know, because it has been a challenge for us to consistently put them to work in our own lives. It takes focus, uncommon discipline, and determined effort. But believe us: it can be done. We know that because we do our best to live the Ally Mindset every day.

Some days are better than others. Some days we're truly 100 percent allies with one another like you wouldn't believe. Maybe even 110 percent. And some days—those days when we're exhausted, frustrated, beat up, torn down—we can't give 100 percent. Maybe we can only give 30 percent of ourselves to becoming better allies; we just don't have any more gas in the tank. And that is 100 percent okay.

If 30 percent is the best you can give at any given moment, then that's great. Keep pushing, keep trying, keep reaching for more.

Keep doing your best.

We're reminded of the fourth agreement—always do your best—from *The Four Agreements* by Don Miguel Ruiz:

Under any circumstance, always do your best, no more and no less. But keep in mind that your best is never going to be the same from one moment to the next. Everything is alive and changing all the time, so your best will sometimes be high quality, and other times it will not be as good. When you wake up refreshed and energized in the morning your best will be better than when you are tired at night. Your best will be different when you are healthy as opposed to sick, or sober as opposed to drunk. Your best will depend on whether you are feeling wonderful and happy, or upset, angry, or jealous.

As we strive to always do our best, we should do everything we can to help our colleagues, clients, friends, family, and others do their best too. As we learned during our COVID-19 days, which have torn many of us out of our offices and isolated us in our homes, this is more important than ever before. We'll ask ourselves, Who needs to hear from me right now? Not in a commercial let-me-sell-you-this-new-thing way, but as a friend, an ally.

It's about connecting, making someone's day a little bit better. It's about the human touch. In a world with so much disconnection, all of us need that touch, whether it's in-person or virtual. Says Eric about a recent client interaction on Zoom,

The last time we talked in-person was when we did a full 360 assessment a year ago. And then we did a handful of follow-up coaching calls, all on the phone during COVID. So, we hadn't seen each other for a year. And when he got on the Zoom video call, the first thing he said was "Man, it is so good to see you." And it just struck me because I thought, "Huh, really? It's good to see me?" He showed up in an Atlanta Braves hat, and we ended up talking about baseball.

I contacted him just to reach out; I didn't need anything from him, and I wasn't trying to sell him something. Even so, three separate times during our conversation, he said something along the lines of "Well, maybe that's an opportunity that you guys can help us with. Maybe you can help us with that."

And I said, "Hey, my intention today was just to check on you. I know there's a ton of stuff going on and that your job has been crazy. I wanted to make sure you were okay."

Again, it's not rocket science. It's common sense. People crave connection, people need connection; it's built deep into our DNA. But we're so busy running on our hamster wheels we forget to reach out.

Relationships are made or broken one conversation at a time. We have a choice to enter into relationships one thought at a time. And those thoughts happen every day. Just because we haven't reached out to someone for six months, that doesn't mean we're bad human beings. It simply means that today we have the opportunity to reach out to someone who needs a human touch. And we can do that starting right now.

Look up. What do you want others to feel in your presence? How do you feel in your own presence?

Show up. Are you intentional about how you show up? Who do you need to connect with?

Step up. There is no try, only do.

And do your best.

Always.

ALLY MINDSET RULES
OF THE ROAD

- **Abundance and generosity** start with *me*. I need to understand and identify my values, goals, hopes, and dreams. Then I can move to you and other key stakeholders who can help me realize them. I am curious about your values, goals, hopes, and dreams, and how they overlap with mine. This is how we get to *we*.

- **Connection and compassion** start with *you*. My motives and intent don't matter if I don't understand where *you* are at. This requires being curious about you, your life story, your experiences, and what you're thinking, feeling, and experiencing right now. Only then can I introduce myself into that equation through compassion and empathy to create amazing results—together.

- **Courage and vulnerability** return to the *me-first* perspective. It is rooted in my own fears and anxieties that may be holding me back—from taking action, having a tough conversation, or moving out of my comfort zone. I can ask you to be my coach, mentor, and ally. Together we strengthen our relationship.

- **Candor and debate** start with *we*—what do you need to know about me, what do I need to know about you, and what do we need to know about the project at hand?

- **Action and accountability** come full circle back to *me*. I must trust that you are going to deliver on your commitments, but I own showing up as the best I can be. I deliver on my expectations so that together we can deliver on the results we have committed to.

ACKNOWLEDGMENTS

WRITING A BOOK *takes a village.*

We have deep appreciation for every single workshop participant, coachee, team leader, executive, family member, friend, colleague, and mentor who has contributed to this body of work. We are honored to have been a part of your leadership journey, and you have made a profound impact on the work we do. We learn from you every single day. This book would not exist without you, and for that, and for you, we are eternally thankful.

We are extremely grateful to Peter Economy who has been a bright guiding light along the way. Your deep commitment to bringing our three perspectives together into one powerful voice in this book has far exceeded our expectations. You have made this process way more fun than it would have been without you!

Thank you to our graphic designers Vicari Vollmar Conley and Jena Persico for visually elevating the work that we do. You continue to inspire us and make everything better.

To Morag's friends and colleagues within the 100 Coaches, especially Marshall Goldsmith—forever an inspiration and now a friend. Linda Sharkey, Beth Polish, Cynthia Burnham, Howard Prager, Deepa Prahalad, Lacey Leone McLaughlin,

Evelyn Rodstein, and many more, who supported Morag every step of the way.

With special thanks to all of our early readers and endorsers: Pamay Bassey; Ayse Birsel; Peter Bregman; Cynthia Burnham; Dorie Clark; Alisa Cohn; Caralyn Cooley; Chester Elton; Dr. Marshall Goldsmith; Adrian Gostick; Mark Goulston, MD; Sally Helgesen; Bob Nelson, PhD; Howard Prager; Garry Ridge; Evelyn Rodstein; Robbie Samuels; Shannon Sisler; Dave Ulrich; Peter Warwick; Charlene Wheeless; and Heather R. Younger.

To the guests on our podcasts, *People First!* and *The Corporate Bartender*, thank you for sharing your leadership journeys with us.

And to all of you who have directly and indirectly contributed to the content in this book—thank you for being our allies!

NOTES

Introduction: Relationships—The True Currency for Success

p. 11   *He made my professional—and personal—life better*: Alison Beard, "True Friends at Work," *Harvard Business Review*, July–August 2020, hbr.org/2020/07/true-friends-at-work.

p. 12   *seven times more likely to be engaged in their jobs*: "What Are Workplace Buddies Worth?" *Gallup Business Journal*, October 12, 2006, news.gallup.com/businessjournal/24883/what-workplace-buddies-worth.aspx.

Chapter 1: The Remarkable Power of Being a Friend at Work

p. 21   *increased our hours in response to the pandemic*: Roy Maurer, "Remote Employees Are Working Longer Than Before," SHRM, December 16, 2020, shrm.org/hr-today/news/hr-news/pages/remote-employees-are-working-longer-than-before.aspx.

p. 22   *committed to their work and workplace*: Gallup Workplace, "What Is Employee Engagement and How Do You Improve It?" accessed March 3, 2022, gallup.com/workplace/285674/improve-employee-engagement-workplace.aspx.

p. 22   *consistently and powerfully link to business outcomes*: Gallup Workplace, "Gallup's Employee Engagement Survey: Ask the Right Questions with the Q12 Survey," accessed March 3, 2022, q12.gallup.com/help/en-us/Answers/164468.

p. 23   *Why do you ask that "best friend" question?*: Rodd Wagner and Jim Harter, "The Tenth Element of Great Managing," *Gallup Business Journal*, accessed March 3, 2022, news.gallup.com/businessjournal/104197/tenth-element-great-managing.aspx.

p. 23   *One company cancelled a 12 Elements survey*: Wagner and Harter, "The Tenth Element of Great Managing."

p. 23   *when employees have a deep sense of affiliation*: Gallup Workplace, "What Is Employee Engagement and How Do You Improve It?"

p. 25   *employees who report having a best friend at work are*: James Harter, Frank Schmidt, Sangeeta Agrawal, and Stephanie Plowman, *The Relationship between Engagement at Work and Organizational Outcomes: 2012 Q12™ Meta-Analysis* (Washington, DC: Gallup Organization, 2013).

p. 26   *Work colleagues matter*: David Ulrich, "Gallup Research Suggests Having a Best Friend at Work Is Critical for Overall Engagement," LinkedIn, linkedin.com/posts/daveulrichpro_gallup-research-suggests-having-a-best-friend-activity-6868966606568075266-L-Le/.

p. 26   *survey of loneliness in the workplace*: Cigna, "Loneliness and the Workplace," accessed March 3, 2022, cigna.com/static/www-cigna-com/docs/about-us/newsroom/studies-and-reports/combatting-loneliness/cigna-2020-loneliness-infographic.pdf.

p. 26   *another survey of loneliness just one year later*: Cigna, "Loneliness and the Workplace."

p. 27   *lonely workers are less engaged and less productive*: Hakan Ozcelik and Sigal Barsade, "No Employee an Island: Workplace Loneliness and Job Performance," *Academy of Management Journal* 61, no. 6 (2018): 2343–66, doi.org/10.5465/amj.2015.1066.

p. 29   *a person is a person through other people*: Angela Thompsell, "Get the Definition of Ubuntu, a Nguni Word with Several Meanings," ThoughtCo.com, September 3, 2019, thoughtco.com/the-meaning-of-ubuntu-43307.

Chapter 2: The Ally Mindset

p. 45   *interacting with their boss is the most stressful part of their workday*: McKinsey & Company, "Five Fifty: Better Bosses," *McKinsey Quarterly*, September 22, 2020, mckinsey.com/business-functions/people-and-organizational-performance/our-insights/five-fifty-better-bosses.

p. 48 *relationships we have with our boss and other managers*: Tera Allas and Bill Schaninger, "The Boss Factor: Making the World a Better Place through Workplace Relationships," *McKinsey Quarterly*, September 22, 2020, mckinsey.com/business-functions/organization/our-insights/the-boss-factor-making-the-world-a-better-place-through-workplace-relationships.

p. 60 *definition used by Nicole Asong Nfonoyim-Hara*: Samantha-Rae Dickenson, "What Is Allyship?" *Communities* (blog), National Institutes of Health, January 28, 2021, edi.nih.gov/blog/communities/what-allyship.

Chapter 3: Abundance and Generosity

p. 67 *Some years ago, I spoke at an educational summit*: Simon Sinek, *The Infinite Game* (New York: Portfolio, 2019), 11.

p. 68 *its people, its community, the economy, the country, and the world*: Sinek, *The Infinite Game*, 13.

p. 68 *the infinite play of life is joyous*: James P. Carse, *Finite and Infinite Games* (New York: Free Press, 2011), 23.

p. 75 *What gets recognized gets repeated*: Dr. Bob Nelson, "How to Bring Employees Back into a Hybrid Workplace," Inc.com, April 2, 2021, inc.com/video/how-the-next-generation-of-female-founders-is-reinventing-leadership.html.

p. 75 *a place of worthiness*: Brené Brown, *Daring Greatly: How the Courage to Be Vulnerable Transforms the Way We Live, Love, Parent, and Lead* (New York: Avery, 2015), 10.

p. 77 *The most powerful words someone can say to you*: Howard Prager, *Make Someone's Day: Becoming a Memorable Leader in Work and Life* (Virginia Beach, VA: Koehler Books, 2021).

p. 80 *In healthy relationships, both people give and receive*: Adam Grant, "In toxic relationships…" Twitter, November 27, 2021, twitter.com/adammgrant/status/1464632416140681225?lang=en.

p. 80 *In grad school, on my first major paper*: Adam Grant, "In grad school…" Twitter, December 20, 2019, twitter.com/adammgrant/status/1208021497761193984?lang=en.

p. 81 *Generosity isn't saying yes to every request*: Adam Grant, "Generosity isn't saying yes to every request…" Facebook, September 1, 2018, facebook.com/488080794576017/posts/2002470663137015/.

p. 81 *The only difference is how you spend that time*: Harry Kraemer, *Your 168: Finding Purpose and Satisfaction in a Values-Based Life* (Hoboken, NJ: Wiley, 2020), 3.

p. 82 *Can competitors be friends*: Ruth Gotian, "If You Want to Succeed, Befriend Your Competitors," Forbes.com, November 23, 2021, forbes.com/sites/ruthgotian/2021/11/23/if-you-want-to-succeed-befriend-your-competitors/.

p. 87 *the league canceled its 2020 season*: Gabe Lacques, "Opinion: Minor League Baseball's Canceled 2020 Season a Cruel Blow in Grim 2020 Sports Year," *Des Moines Register*, June 30, 2020, desmoinesregister.com/story/sports/mlb/columnist/gabe-lacques/2020/06/30/minor-league-baseball-season-canceled-dreams-shattered/3285138001/.

p. 87 *We kept everybody on full pay and benefits*: Jimmy Lynn, "Iowa Cubs Ownership, Front Office Tackle Pandemic-Related Challenges as Fans Return to Principal Park," *Des Moines Register*, May 10, 2021, desmoinesregister.com/story/sports/baseball/iowa-cubs/2021/05/10/iowa-cubs-officials-tackle-pandemic-related-challenges-fans-return-minor-league-baseball-covid-19/5018918001/.

p. 88 *I've got all these great people who work here*: Lynn, "Iowa Cubs Ownership."

p. 88 *Gartner and his associates shared the profits*: Tommy Birch, "Michael Gartner Gave Iowa Cubs Employees $600,000 from the Team's Sale. Here's How It Went Down," *Des Moines Register*, January 3, 2022, desmoinesregister.com/story/sports/baseball/iowa-cubs/2022/01/03/iowa-cubs-owner-michael-gartner-chicago-cubs-alex-cohen-endeavor-diamond-baseball-holdings/9073022002/.

Chapter 4: Connection and Compassion

p. 95 *We are wired for connection*: Brené Brown, *Braving the Wilderness: The Quest for True Belonging and the Courage to Stand Alone* (New York: Random House, 2017), 129.

p. 97 *According to a study of 223 executives*: Constance Hadley and Mark Mortensen, "Are Your Team Members Lonely?" *MIT Sloan Management Review*, December 8, 2020, sloanreview.mit.edu/article/are-your-team-members-lonely/.

p. 98   *Garry shared how the organization shifted its culture*: "Garry
        Ridge, Put People First!" on *People First!* (podcast), produced
        by Morag Barrett, February 28, 2022, 28:38, youtu.be/9d507
        42XG1g.

p. 98   *Our tribe = our success*: WD-40 Company, 2021 *Annual Report*,
        3, s21.q4cdn.com/612895086/files/doc_financials/2021/
        ar/2021-Annual-Report.pdf.

p. 99   *the energy that exists between people*: Brené Brown, "Courage,
        Compassion, and Connection: The Gifts of Imperfection,"
        excerpt from *The Gifts of Imperfection* on Oprah.com, March 12,
        2013, oprah.com/own-super-soul-sunday/excerpt-the-gifts-of-
        imperfection-by-dr-brene-brown/5.

p. 101 *it's because of the power of connection*: Dan Ravid et al., "9 out of
        10 Organizations Are Switching to Hybrid Working, According
        to a McKinsey Survey," World Economic Forum, May 25, 2021,
        weforum.org/agenda/2021/05/executives-future-hybrid-
        work-wfh/.

p. 102 *one in four Americans report having no one*: Allison Sadlier, "1
        in 4 Americans Feel They Have No One to Confide In," *New
        York Post*, April 30, 2019, nypost.com/2019/04/30/1-in-4-
        americans-feel-they-have-no-one-to-confide-in/.

p. 102 *the myopic focus on network size is misguided*: Marissa King,
        Social Chemistry: Decoding the Patterns of Human Connection
        (New York: Dutton, 2021), 11.

p. 102 *Show your people you care about them*: Michelle Tillis Lederman
        quoted in "How to Become a Leader People Want to Follow,"
        Newsweek, September 24, 2021, newsweek.com/how-become-
        leader-people-want-follow-1632409.

p. 104 *If your compassion does not include yourself*: Jack Kornfield,
        Buddha's Little Instruction Book (New York: Bantam, 1994), 28.

p. 104 *a lack of self-compassion affected him*: Aytekin Tank, "Why
        Being Kind to Yourself Is Key to Entrepreneurial Success,"
        Entrepreneur, January 19, 2020, entrepreneur.com/article/
        344920.

p. 110 *trust pervades human societies*: Michael Kosfeld et al., "Oxytocin
        Increases Trust in Humans," *Nature* 435 (2005): 673–6,
        doi.org/10.1038/nature03701.

p. 110 *Paul Zak described the experiment*: Paul Zak, "Trust, Morality—
        and Oxytocin?" TEDGlobal, July 2011, video, 16:18,

ted.com/talks/paul_zak_trust_morality_and_oxytocin/
transcript?language=en.

p. 111   *So we have a biology of trustworthiness*: Zak, "Trust, Morality—
and Oxytocin?"

p. 112   *communication, commitment, competence, and character*: Lolly
Daskal, *The Leadership Gap: What Gets between You and Your
Greatness* (New York: Portfolio, 2017), 165.

p. 116   *the foundations for meaningful connection*: "Dr. Michelle
Johnston, The Seismic Shift in Leadership," on *People First!*
(podcast), produced by Morag Barrett, February 22, 2022,
32:05, youtu.be/3ZnHFIlnxKo.

p. 117   *Research shows that authenticity is strongly associated with*: Anna
Sutton, "Living the Good Life: A Meta-analysis of Authenticity,
Well-Being and Engagement," *Personality and Individual
Differences* 153 (2020): 109645, doi.org/10.1016/j.paid.2019
.109645.

Chapter 5: Courage and Vulnerability

p. 123   *Asking for help is the sign of a secure leader*: Paul Zak, "The
Neuroscience of Trust: Management Behaviors That Foster
Employee Engagement," *Harvard Business Review*, January–
February 2017, hbr.org/2017/01/the-neuroscience-of-trust.

p. 127   *selfish, childish national embarrassment*: Melissa Hernandez
De La Cruz, "In a Sea of Support for Simone Biles, There's
a Razor-Sharp Criticism," *Alive*, July 30, 2021, 11alive.com/
article/sports/olympics/simone-biles-critics-backlash-after-
tokyo-withdrawal/85-bbdc94fa-1189-44b2-a469-7f3af2acf8d7.

p. 132   *73 percent of the population has public speaking anxiety*: John
Montopoli, "Public Speaking Anxiety and Fear of Brain
Freezes," National Social Anxiety Center, February 20, 2017,
nationalsocialanxietycenter.com/2017/02/20/public-speaking-
and-fear-of-brain-freezes.

p. 134   *people prefer their leaders with flaws*: "About Brad D. Smith,"
accessed March 3, 2022, braddsmith.com/about/.

p. 135   *Many of us weren't taught how to express our emotions freely*:
Mark Manson, "Vulnerability: The Key to Better Relationships,"
accessed March 3, 2022, markmanson.net/vulnerability-in-
relationships.

p. 135 *Courage starts with showing up and letting ourselves be seen*:
Brené Brown, *Daring Greatly*, 30.

p. 139 *the more loyal they will be to them*: Emma Seppälä, "Why
Compassion Is a Better Managerial Tactic Than Toughness,"
Harvard Business Review, May 7, 2015, hbr.org/2015/05/why-
compassion-is-a-better-managerial-tactic-than-toughness.

Chapter 6: Candor and Debate

p. 149 *say nothing and keep the peace*: In a LinkedIn article, Morag
shared the emotional leadership crucible that she personally
experienced. See Morag Barrett, "If You Don't Like the Show—
Change the Channel," LinkedIn, November 19, 2020,
linkedin.com/pulse/you-dont-like-show-change-channel-
morag-barrett/.

p. 151 *The ultimate measure of a man is*: "Quotations," National Park
Service, Martin Luther King Jr. Memorial, accessed March 3,
2022, nps.gov/mlkm/learn/quotations.htm.

p. 153 *just one in twenty-five did*: David Maxfield, "How a Culture of
Silence Eats Away at Your Company," *Harvard Business Review*,
December 7, 2016, hbr.org/2016/12/how-a-culture-of-silence-
eats-away-at-your-company.

p. 153 *when a patient's safety is at risk*: Maxfield, "How a Culture of
Silence Eats Away at Your Company."

p. 153 *is at risk of an accident because people don't speak up*: Maxfield,
"How a Culture of Silence Eats Away at Your Company."

p. 155 *create the environment for the conversation that needs to happen*:
"Hope Timberlake, Speak Up Dammit!" on *People First!*
(podcast), produced by Morag Barrett, December 21, 2021,
27:14, youtube.com/watch?v=Ze_qnkdo18w.

p. 155 *First and foremost, candor gets more people in the conversation*:
Jack Welch with Suzy Welch, *Winning* (New York: Harper-
Collins, 2005), 27.

p. 157 *The best managers make a concerted effort*: Jim Harter and Amy
Adkins, "Employees Want a Lot More from Their Managers,"
Gallup Workplace, accessed March 3, 2022, gallup.com/
workplace/236570/employees-lot-managers.aspx.

p. 157 *When you have real trust and respect, candor shows care*: Adam
Grant, "In toxic relationships..." Twitter, February 4, 2022,

twitter.com/adammgrant/status/1489614193988968448?
lang=en.

p. 160 *One of the things we value in our culture is debate*: Tiger
Tyagarajan quoted in Frank Calderoni, *Upstanding: How
Company Character Catalyzes Loyalty, Agility, and Hypergrowth*
(Hoboken, NJ: Wiley, 2021), 177.

p. 161 *Facts don't solve fights*: Liane Davey, "It's the 5th of November!
Today, I'm saying 'NO' to throwing facts at fights…" LinkedIn,
November 5, 2021, linkedin.com/posts/lianedavey_hrvirtual
summit-november-sprinterstribe-activity-68623833988208
55808-H2gQ/.

p. 162 *speak up with concerns, with questions, with ideas, with mistakes*:
Amy Edmondson, "Building a Psychologically Safe Workplace,"
TEDxHGSE, May 5, 2014, video, 11:26, youtu.be/LhoLuui9gx8.

p. 162 *three things you can do to create a psychologically safe workplace*:
Edmondson, "Building a Psychologically Safe Workplace."

p. 170 *To get candor, you reward it*: Welch with Welch, *Winning*, 31.

Chapter 7: Action and Accountability

p. 176 *often misattributed to Einstein*: "Insanity Is Doing the Same
Thing…" Quote Investigator, accessed March 3, 2022,
quoteinvestigator.com/2017/03/23/same/.

p. 183 *If you don't believe the messenger*: James M. Kouzes and Barry Z.
Posner, *The Leadership Challenge: How to Make Extraordinary
Things Happen in Organizations*, 6th ed. (San Francisco, CA:
Jossey-Bass, 2017), 41.

p. 185 *Generosity cannot exist without boundaries*: Brené Brown,
"Boundaries with Brené Brown," The Work of the People, video,
5:40, theworkofthepeople.com/boundaries.

p. 189 *When people overstep, it's not always*: Adam Grant, "When
people overstep…" Twitter, June 5, 2021, twitter.com/
adammgrant/status/1401180474349862919?lang=en.

Chapter 8: From Adversary to Ally

p. 202 *You will get all you want in life if*: Zig Ziglar, *See You at the Top:
25th Anniversary Edition* (New Orleans, LA: Pelican, 2000),
frontmatter.

p. 202 *disrupting businesses everywhere*: Aaron De Smet et al., "'Great Attrition' or 'Great Attraction'? The Choice Is Yours," *McKinsey Quarterly*, September 8, 2021, mckinsey.com/business-functions/people-and-organizational-performance/our-insights/great-attrition-or-great-attraction-the-choice-is-yours.

p. 211 *Recall the results of a 2020 McKinsey survey*: McKinsey & Company, "Five Fifty: Better Bosses."

p. 213 *negative feedback that threatens our self-perception*: Peter Bregman, "13 Ways We Justify, Rationalize, or Ignore Negative Feedback," *Harvard Business Review*, February 14, 2019, hbr.org/2019/02/13-ways-we-justify-rationalize-or-ignore-negative-feedback.

Chapter 9: Trust

p. 230 *threats that CEOs saw to their organizations' growth prospects*: Libby Boswell et al., *24th Annual Global CEO Survey*, PwC Global, 2021, pwc.com/cl/es/publicaciones/pwc-24th-global-ceo-survey.pdf.

p. 238 *conducted a series of field studies*: Daniel Han Ming Chng et al., "Why People Believe in Their Leaders—or Not," *MIT Sloan Management Review*, August 17, 2018, sloanreview.mit.edu/article/why-people-believe-in-their-leaders-or-not/.

p. 239 *It's more difficult to regain credibility*: Chng et al., "Why People Believe in Their Leaders—or Not."

p. 254 *Microsoft reviewed collaboration trends*: Microsoft, "The Next Great Disruption Is Hybrid Work—Are We Ready?" The Work Trend Index, March 22, 2021, microsoft.com/en-us/worklab/work-trend-index/hybrid-work.

p. 255 *When you lose connections*: Microsoft, "The Next Great Disruption Is Hybrid Work—Are We Ready?"

p. 255 *made more challenging in a hybrid environment*: Timothy Bromley et al., "The Great Attrition: The Power of Adaptability," McKinsey & Company, November 22, 2021, mckinsey.com/business-functions/people-and-organizational-performance/our-insights/the-organization-blog/the-great-attrition-the-power-of-adaptability.

p. 256 *reasons why people said they left a job*: Aaron De Smet et al., "'Great Attrition' or 'Great Attraction'?"

p. 256 *reasons why employees decided to stay at a job*: Bromley et al.,
  "The Great Attrition: The Power of Adaptability."

Conclusion: Always Do Your Best

p. 267 *the fourth agreement—always do your best*: Don Miguel Ruiz,
  The Four Agreements (San Rafael, CA: Amber-Allen Publishing,
  1997), 73-74.

ABOUT
THE AUTHORS

Morag Barrett is a highly accomplished keynote speaker, leadership development expert, and bestselling author of *Cultivate: The Power of Winning Relationships* and coauthor of *The Future-Proof Workplace: Six Strategies to Accelerate Talent Development, Reshape Your Culture, and Succeed with Purpose.* Morag is the founder and CEO of SkyeTeam, a boutique leadership development firm, and she has supported more than fifteen thousand leaders from twenty countries on six continents to achieve outstanding results by improving the effectiveness of their leadership and teams.

Morag draws from a deep and unique operational skill set with fifteen years' experience in the finance industry, in addition to more than twenty years of designing and facilitating global leadership and executive development programs. Morag understands the challenges of running a business as well as the complexities of leading and managing the people who are part of that business.

Morag earned a master's degree in human resource management. She is also a recognized business coach for Coach U, a corporate coaching university, and was recently selected from more than sixteen thousand candidates as a top 100 coach by Dr. Marshall Goldsmith, widely recognized as the world's most influential leadership thinker and executive coach.

Morag has contributed to *Entrepreneur*, CIO.com, and the American Management Association. She's also been featured on Inc.com, Business Insider, TheStreet.com, the Association for Talent Development, the Society for Human Resource Management, and HR.com, among others.

For fun, in addition to time with her three sons, you'll find Morag playing the bassoon or ballroom dancing. It's also possible she may simply be relaxing in front of an episode of *Law & Order*. As a footnote, her name is Scottish and means *great*.

Eric Spencer is an HR and leadership development "lifer" who is passionate about helping organizations, teams, and individuals get better. His passion is designing and facilitating executive and leadership development programs that transform careers and leader reputations. As COO for SkyeTeam, he brings more than twenty-five years of experience building and shaping human resources organizations.

Eric holds a bachelor's degree in management from Arizona State University and an MBA with a focus in organizational behavior from Virginia Tech.

He is the father to two amazing young women. As an avid musician, he spends his free time writing, recording, and performing. He's also the host and chief bartender of *The Corporate Bartender* podcast.

Ruby Vesely, CSO for SkyeTeam, is a sought-out executive coach and savvy leadership development expert with more than twenty years' experience in high-tech, nonprofit, and healthcare organizations. Ruby's passion is shaping exceptional organizational cultures, building amazing teams, and ultimately making life lighter at work.

Prior to joining SkyeTeam, Ruby began her career at Seagate Technology as part of a strategic global HR team. Since then, she has worked across industries in organizations of varying sizes and diverse organizational strategies. This collective of experiences helps her quickly learn what makes an organization tick and, from there, build connection and enable leaders and teams to flourish.

Ruby completed her bachelor's degree at Colorado State University and holds a master's degree in organizational leadership from Regis University. She is a certified executive coach (CPCC) and holds the SPHR and SHRM-SCP designations. Ruby is a Colorado native who enjoys biking to local craft breweries with her husband, practicing and teaching yoga, and traveling across the globe for fun adventures!

JOHN A DEMATO, DEMATO PRODUCTIONS

Eric Spencer, Morag Barrett, and Ruby Vesely

WE INVITE YOU TO BE OUR ALLY

Thank you for spending time with us and reading *You, Me, We*. **Please be our ally and write a review online.** It really does help spread the word and we love to read your comments. You can also drop us a note to let us know what most resonated for you: **BetterTogether@SkyeTeam.com.**

Moving from Me to We

Cultivating winning relationships is a powerful experience when your team and organization are all working as allies. SkyeTeam has supported thousands of leaders at all levels in organizations with inspiring workshops, practical tools, and resources that have transformed individual leadership reputations, strengthened team performance, and helped create thriving organizational cultures—places where people want to be and where they can thrive.

If you're ready to accelerate your journey from me to we and bring the concepts in our book to life personally or within your organization, then we're ready to go!

Learn more at **SkyeTeam.com** or contact us directly at **BetterTogether@SkyeTeam.com.**

Ally Mindset Profile

If you haven't already done so, now is the time to complete your personal Ally Mindset Profile. Understand your personal strengths and opportunities in each of the five practices of the Ally Mindset, and then choose from the resources below to support your continued journey. **SkyeTeam.cloud/YouMeWe**

Cultivate the Power of Winning Relationships

If you enjoyed *You, Me, We*, then you will *love* Morag Barrett's book *Cultivate: The Power of Winning Relationships*! In this bestselling book, Morag provides a deeper exploration of the Relationship Ecosystem and the dynamics of four types of relationships: Ally, Supporter, Rival, and Adversary. This book delivers practical tools to navigate every relationship in your career.

Signature Workshop (Virtual or In-Person)

This highly interactive workshop is delivered as a one-day or two-day event that includes a combination of presentation, group activities and discussion, individual reflection, and action planning. A train-the-trainer option is also available.

Keynote Program

Morag Barrett, Eric Spencer, and Ruby Vesely are all-in, ready-to-go event speakers. We're regularly invited to speak at events (virtual or in-person) globally. Our keynotes are interactive and engaging—no talking heads, no death by PowerPoint. Our talks are customized to meet your specific goals and needs, and your leaders will be immersed in discussions and activities that result in real-world application.

Digital Programs

We've created a series of high impact, self-study programs that empower and inspire you to continue your learning beyond the book, keynote, or workshop. These powerful resources include bonus content and videos from us, as well as the practical tools and insights to help you nurture your professional relationships and reputation.

30-Day Professional Relationship Challenge

Join a unique virtual program that brings the concepts from *Cultivate* and *You, Me, We* to life in daily, bite-sized actions. The Relationship Challenge is an immersive way to develop your Ally Mindset and establish healthy behaviors and habits to strengthen your professional relationships. Five minutes per day, five times per week is all it takes to transform and create ally relationships.

Let's talk! We can decide together what the appropriate next steps are. Do contact us to explore your options and confirm availability.

BetterTogether@SkyeTeam.com
SkyeTeam.com
YouMeWeBook.com